Ellie E Johnson

Equestrian Life
The Animal Chronicles

Illustrations by
Jack Murray

For the animals,
With love.

All illustrations are by Jack Murray; Book Design by Dana Dikaitis;
Any photographs are courtesy of the author.

Published in the United States

ISBN 978-0-578-63398-5 (pbk)

1. Horses – Unites States – Anecdotes 2. Horsemen and horsewomen
3. Sporting Life 4. Horsemanship
5. Johnson, Ellie E.

Ellie E. Johnson

CONTENTS

Ellie E. Johnson

Equestrian Life
The Animal Chronicles

"No hour is wasted that is spent in the saddle."

-Winston Churchill

CHAPTER ONE

I Met a Wolf and I Liked It

When I was researching horse camps years ago, I came upon Sans Souci and thought to myself, a horse camp with a name meaning, "No Worries" - Could life get better than that? On my list of camps in the province of Quebec, within an easy drive of Montreal and with a good solid name, it shot to the top of my "favorites". I was ten years old.

Weeks, in truth, half a semester had been spent after school dreaming, planning and trying to find a way to get to a good "horse camp". I didn't even really know what that meant as far as what happened there, but inherent in "horse camp" were "horses" and to me, nothing else mattered. Coming from a non-horsey family, in fact a highly intellectual and rather *anti*-horsey family, I did all the leg work myself and so my parents felt compelled to reward me for my persistence (and nagging) by letting me tour my choice of camp which I had already arranged with a nice woman at "Sans Souci" who was kind enough not to discount a child drilling her with questions over the phone, as a "prank call". So, off we drove one spring afternoon, to the place of multiple horses and no worries.

I remember loving that I had to jump out to open the gate (which kept in horses) before driving down their long, graveled lane bookended by enchanted woods and dark fencing before pulling into park in front of some cabins. It would come to pass that I drove that lane innumerable times for the next eight years and never once lost the feeling of excitement and happiness that bubbled into a quiet smile as I leaned into the proximity of my arrival. That first day, I stepped out onto the laneway and ran ahead of my parents to what appeared to my child self, was a huge barn. My paw on the door to the tackroom, I suddenly heard a booming, cheerful voice behind me. I dropped my hand and turned to see this icon of horsemen. Big smile and hand extended, I met Wolf and it was impossible not to grin back. Years and a good two feet of height set us apart, but I still instantly felt I was more in the right place than I had ever been before. Energy and enthusiasm radiated from his extended hand.

Like the barn, he seemed larger than life. I was awestruck that his "job" was to run this training center. Lucky guy! I grew up in a medical family and Wolf spoke "horse" like I heard "medical" in my house. I liked him immediately. His voice had a great rhythm to it. The kind of rolling rhythm I came to enjoy when I really learned how to sit tall and still while pushing through my horses' extended trots. Accented, rolling, jovial and knowledgeable, it could be soft or extend across multiple fields. I remember my dad winking at me to gauge my reaction and I instantly winked back. The Wolf was good.

This seemingly very tall, active and smart horseman, finished his tour of what my parents were most interested in, facilities, pool, dining room all the while interjecting his experience in Germany with horses and then, he spoke directly to me: "We haven't ever had someone so young call us and set up her own appointment to see the camp. I think Ellie would probably like to see our horses now, is this right?"

I could barely nod. It was RIGHT. My chest pounded. I don't think I drew breath while I listened to Wolf very seriously explain to me what the daily schedule was with barn management, how many hours I would get to ride a day, that I would be responsible for the care of one horse, all to myself, for feeding and grooming. That I would be taught to be a good rider. "And do you know what wolting is?" he asked. Puzzled, I shook my head. "We do lots of wolting!" he said emphatically, like I simply had not lived until I wolted.

"You will do wolting too, on a galloping horse." BIG Wolf-like smile. Vaulting- which, if anyone has seen done well recently, looks like Barnum and Bailey invited Cirque du Soleil to rehearse their entire show on one cantering horse. It is not for the faint of heart. Trying to learn it is exactly the bad end of what you imagine it would be, when you have no idea how to do it. (Poor Tasha, cantering along on a twenty meter circle, had more "roadrunner" outlines imprinted on her side, belly and rear end as children threw themselves every which way at her, trying to get on, hang off, kneel, drag someone else on...In a word..WOLT.) I saw my father's head roll back, his eyes skyward for a second, in the way it did when he was completely defeated. I beamed at him and my mother laughed. Then Wolf, a bear of a man, laughed too. I was sold. And, that was even before I saw the sixty horses.

Much the same as happened with skiing when I wanted to learn and had no choice but to get on a bus alone at seven years old to go to the Laurentians on Saturdays, my parents were a little horrified I was so enthusiastic about going. To overnight camp. With large animals. Far from where they were. I insisted. They tried to gently explain to me that I'd be "alone" at camp. No cell phones back then. It would be carrier pigeon, catch-em-if-you-could, landline communication only. Help was going to be far away. A shy, small child, they tried over and over to gently paint a picture for me. I, however, liked Wolf's picture better. Horses, goats and donkeys to hug and play with? I was IN. There was no actual scenario where this would not be good for me. I knew it at ten and I wasn't wrong.

I heard my parents loud and clear, but I heard Wolf's voice like a dog whistle. We spoke a language on the same frequency. And Wolf spoke to me that day with capital respect for me, for my clear determination to ride and with adult respect for my love of animals. Sans Souci was earning itself another convert.

It was not merely the training I wanted. What I did at that camp was the most fun, most deeply satisfying and important experience in growing to be the accomplished three-day eventer that I eventually became because we experienced all the different ways to ride and partner with your horse. The overnight rides, the lessons, the swimming with horses, the authentic competition every two weeks, the teaching we did, the training of young horses and yes, the competing a few of us were allowed to do but it was more than just that, too.

Sans Souci was a place where people understood a child's will to learn, to love and to grow their real obsession with gorgeous, kind equestrian athletes. It was a place to learn responsibility for beings other than yourself. It was a place where you got out as much as you put in and at an age when you didn't even realize what value that held. It was a place where Wolf would have you galloping bareback over cross country fences in the dead of winter with your best friends, jumping higher every round and making you and your horse feel like it was the best idea ever to be jumping four feet in a blizzard when you finished. (Don't try this at home.) He built trust, bravery and commitment between horse and rider.

His wife, Ann, always had an eye out for children who might need a hug or a kind word in a solitary moment.

It taught me to love community, work at friendships and respect creatures great and small. It was a place where I wasn't alone in my adoration of horses and my interest was coddled and nurtured with friends in fun and adventures whenever I was there. Fun, kind and trusting, Wolf also pushed children to trust themselves. I wouldn't say it was Lord of the Flies, but we were allowed to learn through error too, most of it smartly hidden from Wolf. I became very familiar with the cautionary phrase, "discretion is the better part of valor!"

The community that Wolf and Ann built is hard to repeat. They spoke to their little riders like little adults and were interested in what we had to say. We were encouraged to push our limits as riders and as horsemen/women, which paid off in the type of bravery and comfort with speed and distance that is impossible to teach to upcoming "indoor arena" riders. What made him riveting as a first coach, beside his big voice and big presence, was his product. There was nothing more that I enjoy, even to this day, than to get to the end of a beautiful summer's day having accomplished my own targets for riding and be able to sit down and watch better riders than I, train with their equine partners. At ten, I had watched Wolf helping his daughter win events all around Quebec on her fabulous grey gelding, Julius Caesar. The image of an excellent rider on her gorgeous knee-snapping grey, thundering across fields over all or any cross-country fences in their way, made me an eventer. It made me a horsewoman. It made me a trustee of horses.

I had been riding since I was three when I found "No Worries", multiple horses, multiple dear friends, a correct riding seat and beaming joy. To finally (at ten years old) find a place where I could stay and ride for weeks at a time, riding, learning and playing with horses and friends just like me, was a brand-new world. It was also the beginning of realizing a lifelong passion and extended career with horses which even as a working MBA, I am still involved with to this day.

As an adult, I can't express how many times I've heard "I was so lucky to have a passion". It took me a few years to be self-aware enough to understand how it can drag you forward through life's challenges and repeated tasks! How it lands you on the parallel journey of efforts to be excellent in every channel in life; We strive to be the best riders, human beings, trainers and trustees to our equine partners that we can be and not necessarily in that order. What they were saying too is, "you are so lucky to have a 'happy place'". What I'd say, is that I was blessed. A lot of the passion originated with Wolf's kindness, respect and interest in little people who wanted to learn what he wanted to teach. One simply cannot bottle the magic many of us felt growing up with purpose and fun in equal measure at his farm.

If you want to be a great rider, learn to play with your horses. It's good for them. It's good for you and it's vital to you both as a team. Even until recently, I always handled my own horses, groomed them, dressed them, undressed and treated them myself. It is my temple, that intimate, quiet barn time. It's our friendship time when we are equal and not trainer and student. (The learning goes both ways, as my horses like to remind me.) It is our "quality time". The practice of recognizing the feel of your horse, the growth of a laser-like eye that unconsciously studies every hair on their body for change, the ebb and flow of their energy, the observance of the way they move, stemmed from my learned love and discipline of caring for my horses, of being thoughtful of them. Being a great horseman is a journey and it started with brushing my horse three times a day at Sans Souci.

And lastly, on a personal note, vaulting back up on a galloping horse between penalty zones (back when we had them) if you had been tossed cross country, or if a baby had offed you in the stable yard or even just hacking bare back and being bucked off, saved a lot of time. The "wolting" really paid off!

"Excellence is the gradual result of always striving to do better."
-Pat Riley, NBA head team coach, Miami Heat, LA Lakers and New York Knicks.

CHAPTER TWO

Cross Country Luncheon

There are transcendent benefits to high risk sports. The experience of devoting oneself to excellence in something very hard, changes you. As I have grown through sports and business over thirty years, I inevitably get asked about my motivation to pursue high risk sports. Downhill ski racing and Three Day Eventing, in my case, but open water kayaking, cliff jumping, surfing et al. for multiple others. The short answer, of course, is that they are fun. It wasn't until I was older that I realized I had a much-augmented answer to give now, provided by psychologists who have finally been studying the more complex reasons of extreme sport motivation.

They have dug a little deeper into the topic of why some people pursue sports known to be more dangerous than others and provided more material and genuine data than all the usual fluff out there about inane sensation-seeking or risk-taking that actually, never crossed my mind at three years old when I sat on my first pony.

Interestingly, there is truly a movement to individual performance in sports and away from group sports; a lot of more learned people than I concur that people enjoying upper level competition in a high-risk sport, don't consider themselves to be high-risk lunatics. There are easier ways to go, that will save you oodles of time and money if that is your quest. These researchers have also gratefully debunked the routine assumption that something is just "wrong with these people," a slur which is patently untrue. Mostly. They don't consider their sports risky, generally, although they are amply aware of what their lack of focus or study can cost them. But riders are not BASE jumpers or pro climbers who we sadly see eulogized by the thousands every year. Riders are doing what every Tom, Dick or Harriet would do in the 19th Century for transportation. It's the eventers who are the BASE jumpers. (Not true. No one in their right mind would do that.)

For the sport and our beloved animals, having people who love horses and dogs partake in hacking, schooling or simply riding into the further stretches of open space, enjoying nature with their partners, is what grows our sport and our respect for our animals as well as our environment. Competitors, however, are at a higher level of pursuit and in a race with themselves.

If you ask athletes what draws them to high risk sports, I think it's been clearly documented that having a screw loose mentally is not in the top ten of their answers. Much clearer heads choose to pursue perfecting one's self, one's skills and your horse's while you are still able to supplely use your body. What was, however, in every athlete's top two answers was their liking, passion and respect for how *hard* their sport really is, how hard the endeavor of being excellent, really is. And, *that* is what they enjoy.

It is the daily grind of infinitesimal improvement, the quest to acquire the highest levels of knowledge and experience that will very deliberately shave off larger and larger chunks of risk, that drive most extreme athletes. The more you study, the more you learn, the less the risk. The feeling athletes try to describe in whatever risky sport they do, and what they describe when forced to offer up something more personal than "fun" in several surveys, is that they are more authentically themselves, closer to nature, more self-aware and counter-intuitively, more at peace. It's not just a few seconds of rush. Thankfully, research and findings of extreme athlete motivation are now more available and we no longer have to be dismissed as adrenaline-junkies, freaks or wastrels, descendant from a genotype that screams "Death First" before our first cup of coffee.

Having said that, those quests for excellence are not for everyone. There are several people I know who are more than accomplished at riding or white river rafting or mountain climbing who choose to stay at a high level of accomplishment and hold. Base camp is fine and summiting can wait. They have found their own acceptable, correct ratio of knowledge to risk and are happy in their spot. Besides, it is the beginnings of any such learnings that will kill you, not pursuing it once you've spent years in practice.

It was when I was retired from competition and not sitting on a horse at all, that my moments of "learning" came back to me with much more clarity and I relived them with friends one day, on a late summer's afternoon.

White tent flaps billowed in the breeze as I ducked into the hospitality lunch of the local annual horse show, late. Friends waved from our table and I snaked my way through a packed buffet line headed in their direction, one eye on the horses already competing around the hunter course. It's nice to occasionally just watch, enjoy the spectacle and be clean around horses!

I slipped into my white folding chair and unfurled my napkin in perfect sync with a competitor who was also soaring sharply into the air, parting ways with her handsome horse and jettisoning into my peripheral vision. I winced. My shoulders snapped back in empathy, willing her back in the tack, but to no purpose.

As elegant as you might try to make the landing, the turf was soft and she torpedoed through it, arms and chest divoting her path, to land with a jarring thud not five feet from my chair. Where moments before, the buzz in the tent had been audibly cheerful and ricocheting pings of laughter alternated with the announcer on the loudspeaker, in a second, stillness. Wait staff held serving spoons at the buffet in mid-air. My napkin waved in the soft breeze, my arm still suspended before reaching my lap.

The fingers of her beautiful, butter-colored string gloves instantly blackened and her helmet turned brown with a nice grass stain crowning the left side. We all held our breath.

Slowly, her head lifted. Much like a grey after a muddy turnout day, the only thing we saw in her face were her eyes when they snapped open. Her fingers flexed carefully in the dirt taking stock of her working limbs. With a good head shake, more dirt flew and then, with the nimbleness of youth, she leaped to her feet. Straightening her helmet, she dusted off her breeches, adjusted the cuffs of her riding shirt under the dirty sleeves of her black jacket and looked insouciantly around for her horse. Jane Bond. The crowd burst into relieved and happy applause. A big grin and a bow to the crowd and off she strode to collect her partner.

I grinned. "Ah, yes, I remember it well!"

While stewards ran to help her reconnect with her beautiful bay, now near the ingate and bucking ecstatically around the field in his own personal victory gallop, I resumed my greetings and leaned over to give a hug to a good friend whom I was happily surprised to see at the table.

"Ohhhh, that poor girl," Gordon said sweetly. "Ellie, what do you think happened?" he asked earnestly while the rest of us still chuckled in sympathy.

"I think we call it stickability, Gordon. Somedays you've got it and others...You know, riding isn't as easy as it looks! Practice makes perfect and that looked like a naughty youngster who didn't have his attention on his job and neither did his pilot. They will do better next time. She might need a new pair of gloves, but I think she's ok." I winked at him to alleviate his worry.

Gordon smiled and then looked thoughtful again. "I guess falling happens. Poor her." Gordon had ridden all through his middle age. I squinted an eye at him, trying to discern if he had forgotten falling.

'It happens to the best of us,' I laughed. "When Podge was a 4-year-old, I did a compete flip over her head when she jammed the brakes on in one of these classes. I could hear my friends roar from across the field! I landed on my feet, on the other side of a tiny oxer with a very scary flower box, staring her right in the face, still holding her reins. I took a bow to big applause and got back on to finish my round. Somedays, winning looks differently than you'd imagine. Having all your limbs intact is a blue ribbon start on one's gratitude list. It means you'll live to fight another day!" The whole table laughed in agreement.

Gordon was 92 years old. A repository of riding history in our town and now widowed and alone, he had first been "adopted" by a good friend of mine who devoted her time and resources to making his days better. When we met a few years back at a holiday party at her house, we'd become fast friends and he'd been enriching our lives ever since with his stories. He was still a recorder of history and had a magical eye for reproducing what he saw in art. He had come out to enjoy the weather, color, pageantry and talent of some of the local riders at the horse show, not to mention a pretty good lunch. There was nothing he loved more.

"You mean this has happened to you, too?" he seemed shocked. "When you were eventing?"

I nodded. "Yes, and we train separately too in three disciplines so, having a show jump or hunter show in our backyard means you take full advantage!"

'Right! I used to go to the events in town and watch too. It's amazing and so exciting when it's done well."

I grinned. "We certainly aim to do it well. If you don't it's a LOT more exciting..."

"Are there more falls do you think?" he asks earnestly.

My other riding friends at the table howled with laughter, their own experiences with acrobatics off their horses never forgotten. How to answer that without horrifying people. Too casual and it seemed all we did was fall, which of course, we did not. Too mute and it discredits the determination and toughness required to win, as any fall at pace is a little more spectacular. In truth, when my horses matured past their novice and training stages, we never had one fault cross country for the rest of their careers other than time faults and I never fell unless they did (knock on wood), having had a great coach who drilled us on position, position and more position.

However, riders do fall. Not a lot if you are going to stay in for the long game. But, it's part of the business of trying to align yourself with a 1200 pound, super athletic and highly independent athlete who will become the best relationship you will have in your life if you are lucky, or the worst. Some wisely cut their journey short or should, if the latter.

Becoming an excellent rider is a large ambition. Some enjoy it with full knowledge that the pot of gold is spread all along the rainbow. It's their church, their wellbeing and their privilege. Some ride a shooting star and stop and yet others will hang on too long. The "pot" is always just icing on the cake. It's the relationships, the achievement of excellence, the love of the horses you never forget.

Great riders walk tall as trees and they are determined to keep their view. Others persevere past their physical ability to keep up and begin to show signs of fraying. Just like in life, there is a fine line mentally between perseverance and unhealthy persistence and we pray to keep the clarity of seeing both. Hence, also hopefully avoiding the "sensation-seekers" moniker.

Keeping it light, I responded: "Gordon, eventers have three different ways to learn how to be turfed. And three different ways to learn to stick. We practice show jumping and dressage not just to win but because it is also so important to being excellent cross country. It builds the strength, agility and adjustability our horses need to succeed at speed coming into large, unmoving obstacles. I personally think though, that enduring, passionate, good or bad partnerships are cast while riding across country."

"Oh dear," Gordon said thoughtfully, "You are going a lot faster cross country, aren't you? Falls must be worse."

I grinned. "Occasionally! I've seen some good ones show jumping, or playing polo or out hunting, too. Whenever you jump, you can also miss."

Horses are the great equalizer. They keep you humble. You can think positively and sometimes deservedly that you were going to be great on any given day, training had gone well, horse feeling super and BAM! They just sit you down with the owner's manual again. So, achieving the perfect show jump round or an enviable dressage ride or the holy grail of all three phases going well at an event, is a constant pursuit.

Less fun had been a time when I did fall, still on the sharp incline of my learning trajectory when I was concussed and lost my memory for a year. I wasn't going to bring that up though, in public! Memory unbidden, when for a year, I had to hunt for every single one. Life's little ironies, my mother would say.

It had been on a horse I took as a project and yes, we were going way too fast. Bolting is always too fast. It was a schooling day and the horse wasn't a great jumper and he did what he actually was good at, which was to not jump and he did it by inverting his back, throwing his head in the air in panic and bolting straight into an oxer with no instigation from me. I was so concentrated on not reacting to his panic, fully expecting him to lower his head without someone yanking on his mouth, that it never occurred to me to pull away. Lessons learned.

He ended up folded nicely like a deer sleeping on top of the oxer and was fine. I came off like a javelin thrown by

Ashton Eaton on his way to winning gold in the decathalon in 2016. The thought of it still made my neck hair stand up and to be honest, I only remember what I was told after the fact. Yup, that was a good, speedy fall.

At the same farm, when an event was officially running, my coach was not going very fast at all in a show jump warm up area when the resale horse she was training got a show jump rail between his front legs on take-off and they parted company. I can distinctly remember being across a field and still hearing her threaten the EMTs with physical harm if they cut her thousand dollar boots off. Yup, those were the days! When people spoke of "dying with their boots on," they weren't just talking about the military.

"Gordon," I finally replied, 'It really depends on how you fall. If you fall with your horse which happens rarely, that's no joke." Being a projectile missile with a 1200 pound horse curled around you is no laughing matter. Being thrown clear has its advantages if you have a little pace. The more common ones are medium paced training blurbs like we all have when one tumbles off without being catapulted anywhere. You pop out of the tack, but generally are no worse for wear. Somewhere in the middle is what we just saw. It would have been ungenerous to mention that thankfully, other than that good concussion, I had not had many falls at all - that were worth mentioning - that I had the time to tell. The luncheon wasn't itself, a three-day event.

There had been one or two nice rides around the hunter course now and people were starting to re-focus on seconds at the buffet and touching base with friends at other tables. The hum resumed. Gorgeous sun, light wind, horses and riders and friends, it was a great way to spend a Sunday afternoon.

Gordon asked: "Don't you ever get scared galloping fast at obstacles that don't move on cross country?"

I smiled broadly, "I'm pleading the fifth, but I would say that some nerves keep you sharp, focused and in the zone.

Scared? No. Excited and focused, yes. I actually find watching someone else have a bad go to be more distressing."

I was pondering how hard we used to train and work at being excellent horsemen and riders. It was all consuming and our gang of friends who all trained together were excellent athletes and riders. It's why I loved our town. Back then, it was a mecca of superior horsemanship and we were taught by the best to be our best. We were so lucky.

Gordon nodded, "Yes, that is bad. I don't think we have time to think when it's happening to ourselves but watching is hard."

'Yes. My dad wouldn't watch cross country again for a couple years after my head injury. My mum was very brave and she'd always stay for all three phases, but my dad would re-appear for show jumping."

Before I moved further south on the east coast though, I rode and eventually taught at a horse camp. I was occasionally allowed to go off to competitions with another instructor, my friend Ben, who also loved eventing and off we'd go, no coach, barely of driving age, not knowing what you don't know, but badly wanting to event. As can sometime happen, we had a really bad day.

Not a bad 'I-left-a-piece-of- equipment-or-clothing-at-home' kind of day, but a 'where-is-my-Job-t-shirt, I'm in hell,' kind of day. And it had started out so happily. Both good riders but not loaded with show experience yet, Ben and I were off to an event in a small town driving a farm rig and two horses, so excited to go to the show. Looking back, I wouldn't even load a motor bike into what amounted to an old steel step up trailer which we had to use then. Unloading when we arrived, a lead-line got caught in one of the ancient door hinges of the trailer and my horse pulled back lifting the entire top door up and away with him. It landed on my head. Out like a light.

Wow, riders are good looking! I opened my eyes to the urging of a tall, dark and yes, handsome rider asking me if I was ok. Ben was holding my horse and I had no idea what had happened. Like all good riders, pride drove me to my feet and I got up mildly nauseated with a cracking headache but went on to compete. I could have played femme fatale with the gorgeous man trying to help me but my vanity shot me upright, regardless of how many of him I could see. I made it through dressage, poorly, and around cross country clear but with time and went walking back to the start box after caring for my horse, to watch Ben go.

Ben rode one of the toughest horses in the camp. Stinger was well named and while I have so much affection and loyalty for camp horses who just give their best to little monsters learning not to bounce and bang all over them, Stinger made good sport of keeping the plebian equestrians at bay. If you were witless and a good rider, the occasional camper would try to get through a lesson with him but Ben was about the only one who could ride him well. All that to say that Stinger liked Ben just as well before as after he rolled on him, over the first fence on course, trying his hardest to refuse and being thwarted by Ben's vice like legs.

What I saw, from a distance was Stinger napping like a champion as he left the start box. One stride canter, pop, rear, twist, canter two strides, trot stare at the trailers, twist, canter... I stopped walking, eyes like golf balls, willing them on. "Go forward!" I was shrieking in my head.... but in seconds I was going forward, in full run, pain shooting through my head, watching them drip and drag over the large log and flip onto the other side with Ben disappearing from view into the soft turf. I 'm pretty sure if I had been the rider or coach I am now, that would not have happened, but two sixteen-year-old kids were then at an event having a hell day, with no support. We still had to get the horses home too.

Running harder, I saw Stinger leap to his feet like he'd merely dropped to the ground for a good roll, which indeed, he had and then, Ben. Ben rolled right up after him. He was clutching his left arm, covered in dirt but he snatched the reins before Stinger could even think of going anywhere, stuck his boot in the stirrup and was up and away before any officials could stop him. Clear the rest of the round. Even I had my jaw slack. Nowadays, you are instantly eliminated if you fall. And people still wonder the merits of that rule. Not I! I also understand better why people think we are "sensation-seekers" or are of some gene mutation. Not at all, this was simply part of our early learning curve in a high-risk sport.

I don't think we lingered for show jumping and on the way home with the horses happily chomping on hay in the back, I remember a lot of: "Ellie, can you reach my sunglasses for me? My arm..." and "Ben, turn down the radio can you? My head..." Plenty of moans of "Don't make me laugh, it hurts!" all the way home with a busted arm and a concussion. It's great to be young...and still alive.

It is hard to explain to people who do not like to ride, the love that is inherent in good partnerships. The bond that brings you back over and over, that overrides disappointment, that allows you to look "outward and forward" to the next great ride because every experience is honing a better one for the next time. In some of us, the magnetic pull of working at something to just get better every single day is I think, what is described routinely in job requirements as "self-motivation". In others, the pull is just pure, unadulterated love for horses, their minds, hearts and senses of humor. For me, it is both.

The passion of loving horses and being a good athlete translates into multiple languages: work ethic, family, environment and animal welfare. The language of humane. The language of besting yourself. The language of winning. All in the dialect of "we never give up." One came to learn also that without due thoughtfulness, never giving up could also get you hurt in our sport. More hurt. Sometimes in show jumping, rarely in dressage, but definitely on cross country. Persistence is vital but introspection and intelligence about your physical and mental abilities are vital too.

"Cross country is very different, isn't it, from show jumping, different from hunting too, wouldn't you say?" Gordon sat sipping tea into his frail body as we happily had one eye on the competition and another on our salads and chatting.

"Yes. I'd definitely say." I grinned at him. "Firstly, I like one-to-one activities. For example, tennis vs squash. Who wants to be on the same side of the net trying to dodge a high velocity racquet swing while you lunge to get to the ball? Not me." I know I can be razor focused on the win. I'd be into those racquet heads and probably deaf, blind and cheekbone-less, in no time. That is fox hunting.

Stick with what you know, I say. Hunting with several horses, some not manned particularly expertly after flasks of wine and good "hooch" at every hold, all trying to jump together across a coup sitting slope down in bad footing is more horrifying to me with my competition horses than jumping the coffin at Ledyard. On a donkey. In a blizzard. Blindfolded. But, a ton of fun the few times I have been generously offered a horse to go on!

Secondly, show jumping happens in a ring, the fences fall down and you jump approximately a third of the fences you jump cross country at a third the pace. It's an art to be mastered in its own right and some hu-normous height to the jumps too. Speed is definitely involved as is good timing, but just slightly less likely to make you pay for an error by launching you further than the walls of the arena that confine you. But who thinks of all this when choosing an equestrian discipline? That's right. No one.

Being alone on course, though, is not to say eventing is easier than hunting, for instance. Quite the opposite. It is a competitive sport versus a social one and it requires honing of all your skills every day to be good. Some people are lucky enough to have a horse who loves hunting and they also have their performance horses to ride so they are adept at all disciplines! It all requires great partners.

I thought of my Big Blue, kind-hearted, funny, elegant and a thinker. Cary Grant. Hugely talented. It's not like the sport isn't tough enough, but sometimes, you can also just get the bad end of a stick by chance, like I did in Georgia one year finding myself the first horse out on cross country, running over a huge preliminary/intermediate course after a hurricane had blown through the afternoon before. The footing was *not* good.

This would be far less intimidating for a show jump round. But on that day, I could have run like we had something to worry about, or as my coach would have told me, I could just do my job, give Blue confidence, keep him packaged and get to it. Blue got to it and while I knew they were announcing every single jump into stabling over the loud speaker and that everyone was listening to how the course was riding, my boy was thundering into huge triple bar logs, shortening into combos and lifting us out of the mud like it wasn't there, cruising where it was safe to eat up ground and listening every step of the way. It wasn't always pretty and I knew he was working hard in places, so we just went slow. I have a great picture of him from that event, clearing the first of two huge boat docks by a foot, knees tight, me quietly folded on his back, about three from home. A lot of people had much less successful rides that day. Turns out, in horrible footing, it's not the worst thing in the world to go first! We were lucky. And careful. And gave heart to the eighty or so of my brethren who were waiting post hurricane, to see if Blue made it around the course clear, so they could decide whether to run themselves or not.

"Yes, cross country is very different than show jumping or hunting," I replied with a smile.

There is and should also be, additional pressure on riders with smart, loving partners in most cases, who trust you to be good, ethical captains and to react well to whatever kind of day you will both have, given a thousand inputs. That day, we just wanted to get around, go slowly, take jumps from the best place for him to adjust to the mud, move on where the footing might be good, but get a good start to the event day and above all come home with him safely. They know when it's a tough day. They know. And, if you've put in not just the

·technical work but the relationship work, they dig in and make things happen for you.

No one was more proud of themselves returning back to stabling than Blue. Striding along, noseband flapping, girth loose, cloaked like the champion he really was in his fancy cooler, he had clamped my sleeve in his teeth, jigging here and there, bumping me occasionally with his shoulder or nose, frisking my pockets for raisins, all the way to stabling. Strolling down the aisle to be cared for, he swung his long neck left and right as he passed his stable mates and our friends, all calling: "Yeah, Blue!" Vinny Barberino at the disco. Happy, funny boy. Talented boy. He made me shine against a vast pool of elite competitors with much more pocket and experience than we had. But who ever thinks of that when you are chasing your life's dream? Yup. No one.

I always kept a spare blue ribbon in the trailer tackroom for that one. If he wasn't in the ribbon ceremony after show jumping, which he usually was, he was devastated. Really. The first time it happened, I thought he was colicking, he was so desolate. It was truly unusual, so I just made sure he always got rewarded for his talent and effort. He deserved a ribbon every day, let alone after an event! And so, he got one.

Blue is frozen in my head for a minute, ears pricked happily forward, way up-in-the-air over the boat dock, in perfect, eternal flight. Pegasus. A star. A best friend. My heart swells at the memory of the horse who placed all over the United States and Canada, teaching me to be a great competitor, teaching me how to ride dressage well and how to fight for show jumping points. But mostly, he taught me to see distance at speed and to soar over big, huge jumps, ditches, steps and water with confidence, just like we do in non-riding life. A Godsend of talent to a child who had dreamed of his likeness exactly since she was 3 years old. Every single day I placed a boot in a stirrup on that horse, I was aware of how special he was. I remain grateful to this day for our partnership.

After considering all this, I smiled at Gordon, "Cross country is a platform where you and your partner will wake naturally a little different every day and try to keep the same safe level of communication between you to vanquish multiple variables at speed, over changing terrain and in all kinds of weather. Mostly, it's just screaming good fun. The biggest fun I know." I grin hugely.

The wind is on your face, your horse and you are one soaring over fences and the feeling of happiness, partnership, accomplishment and freedom are almost indescribable. Riders know it. The horses know it. It's the exam at the end of semester before Christmas break. It's the best of highs on the up and down trajectory of life, when battling through lows necessitates a little relief. Some people get that gardening. Whichever way you need it, you should get it, but loving horses and experiencing their magic is nirvana to a horse person.

The pursuit of excellence is the win. It tells you something about yourself. It tells your horse something about you. The better you are, the more you can do with your horses. It's also the spirit of continuity from a different age when what we do in the present reminds us of what was urgently required of our military in the past. It's teacher and parent. It's a microcosm of life and an enormously difficult task to master well.

"What are you two yakking about over there?" one of my friends bellows over the lunch buzz.

Gordon and I both replied in unison: "Jumping!!"

Gordon's ninety-year-old eyes sparkled brightly in his smiling face. "And, perfect partners! Cross country freedom!" he added.

I grinned and bobbed my head. 'Worth a little turf in the face, too, on occasion. Freedom comes at a price." I winked at him.

With lunch finished, we all continued to enjoy the lovely horse show rounds outside our tented dining room in the field, providing audience to the ones in the arena, giving it their all on a sunny, early autumn's day, when only those with a screw loose would think of doing anything else.

Ellie E Johnson

"Once you have had a wonderful dog, a life without one, is a life diminished."

-Rudyard Kipling

CHAPTER THREE

Scents and Sensibility

In horse racing, winning by a nose can be the difference between a Triple Crown Winner, revered and recorded forever in the annals of history or the blind disrespect of anonymity that will follow champions like Smarty Jones (2004) or Big Brown (2008) forever. Impressive, exceptional runs winning two legs of the largest horse racing event in the world, but a miss in the third, loss by merely a nose in some cases, and that's where their glory ends. A miss is a miss, but by a nose is devastating. It can break the hearts of the toughest competitors. Conversely, win by a nose and it might as well be a mile.

The most elite of wine tasters will also tell you that looking at a glass of wine for color then swirling a glass of wine to agitate it allows its aromas to blossom and are two important steps in learning to appreciate an excellent wine or discern a "corker". The nose, however, is everything. A taster will finally smell before tasting in order to prepare the brain for a more complete tasting experience. The more smells a nose knows, the more layers it differentiates in a good wine.

Humans have two odor detecting patches high up on their nasal passages. They can detect thousands of different smells through five or six million of these yellowish cells sitting up high and back in the nose canal. A dog, though, has anywhere from two hundred and twenty (220) to three hundred (300) *million*. They are housed in parcels that if removed and unfolded, would be the size of a fully laid out handkerchief compared to the Post-It note size of ours. So, when you are discouraged your buddy isn't grasping the finer points of finding his ball or toy or even your spouse, it isn't because he can't nor that he isn't a blood hound. The flesh must be willing.

A good trailing dog can catch scent from a mile away. Five times further than a human. All those little skin particles we shed regularly? Food aplenty to a trailing dog. Smells swirl too. Swirling isn't good for dogs. Straight edging is good. In humans, we smell coffee in the morning and it activates our smell neurons. The brain does something with that to translate it into the thought, "coffee", but it's hard to pinpoint precisely what those actions are.

A dog can smell something and a lot goes on in his brain before it provokes his response and when it does, say trigger my likeness to him, he can have a variety of reactions. For instance, I can deliver my shepherd to his nanny, leave on a trip and be certain to hear one of my dog's reassuring behaviors from her by bedtime. I leave things with him with my scent in the event he is looking for a little comfort. When he finds them, his long tail sweeps back and forth, headfirst in his overnight bag, retrieving one of my shirts.

I never tell anyone what "tells" my dog will show. The report I get is more authentic then and I get a better picture of what is going on. It could also be said that I'm a little more interested in how my animals communicate than some. Or that translating responses from them has been like elementary English to me since I was two years old. You'd imagine a clinical, scientific and cold head would accompany all these animal observations. In reality, that is the least way to observe anything of real depth in creatures that thrive like we do, in family.

I treat my dogs as if my inadequate time for working with them is vastly superseded by their capacity for learning. They get the benefit of the doubt. My current shepherd reminded me of my unintentional disrespect early on in our relationship. I made the error of repeating the "bring me the ball" lesson pedantically, slowly and with, I am ashamed to say, a bad attitude for probably 30 minutes one day. The first two times, he sat solemnly and watched me. His eyes lit up briefly at the ball, but he was motionless. Then he lay down. I sighed. He groaned. I rolled my eyes once or twice at his seeming indifference. I eventually sat down too, before renewing my efforts instead of quitting for the day or just moving on to something he wanted to learn. My interest almost as low as his, I stared at him, lying on the carpet, his gold eyes on me with zero expression.

My previous shepherd was my heart's beat. Impressively intuitive, alert and working 24/7, he shadowed me, smartly protective and brilliant, never slept while I waked, knew with a chin lift what I was talking about. A kindred spirit. I looked at Artemus. I just didn't see this three-year-old colossus, a rescue, uneducated and emaciated, as working his way to that level, no matter how well bred he was or perhaps because of it.

"Wow. We are both sad. Not good," I mutter into his flat eyes. "We'll call it for today. You're free to go, man." I add with a self-amused laugh, like telling a pet rock to "sit". Artie's flat eyes never changed in his handsome face while he stood up and walked slowly into the living room, climbed up on his bed and went to sleep. It snapped my laughter right out of the air. I felt my eyes round then narrow. "Hmmm, interesting timing. The BSO called and wants you back." I mutter, watching him for a second.

A couple days went by and Artemus settled into his early morning exercise schedule, sorted out when I leave for work, that he had to have breakfast before I go, knew to expect his dog walker mid-day and when to expect me home again. We hadn't had much time to play ball when he needed to learn every one of a hundred details of just co-existing with his human easily. I continued in observation mode, letting him tell me his story organically. Just walking him was exhausting since he had no idea what a leash was and flung himself around like a ninety-pound kite. His arrival had coincided with the backend of my recovery from shoulder surgery too, so I was still a little leery of falling, even months after the fact. One afternoon, when I almost twist my ankle on one of Artie's unused tennis balls in the kitchen, I pick it up and fling it lightly down the hall out of the area and almost instantly regret it since I'll forget it's there and undoubtedly, fall over it again later.

I laugh as I look over at Artie, watching me prepare food that I will have to beg him to eat as I do three times a day, and say, " Hey, can you make yourself useful buddy? Bring me that ball." Cracking myself up. Artemus gets up, gives me a full-on stink eye and walks calmly down the hall. I dropped what I had in my hands to follow him, pretty sure he may have been on his way to act-out his dirty look for me and stopped in my tracks.

I watched as he leaned into a corner, extending his long spine, head low, then backed up like an 18-wheel rig, very carefully turning with a yellow ball in his mouth. He stared at me a beat then walked up to me and spat it out onto my feet before carrying on to lie back down. I cocked my head sideways at him and narrow my eyes. He hasn't broken my stare. My eyes dip to my feet and back to Artemus, watching me calmly, sure his lot in life has been to be saddled with the slowest human known to dogs. His eyes were disgusted. "Got it on the second go. Have no idea what you were doing the other 30 times."

"Roger that," I mutter. "Sorry."

Artie also had some other tells. The one night he spent away from home, his nanny tried to lure him to bed by bringing him his overnight bag. She opened it and without skipping a beat, he politely got up, forced her hands away, dove into the bag and took out a flannel shirt I had packed for him and lay down on it, turning away from her, eyes closed instantly. He wasn't sleeping.

He wasn't comforted with my scent, he was worried I was gone. He didn't want her to touch his stuff. Muddy the waters, so to speak. Our reaction to the same things, scents, memories can be very different. I learned that having him at home, surrounded by his and my things always made a difference to him. In his mind, one scenario meant it was possible *he* wasn't returning to me and the other meant *I* was definitely returning to him. He stays home now. Always. Rescues, like a box of chocolates...

Huck, my previous shepherd, was an 'ear' dog. Good nose but GREAT ears. Artie is good ears but the top "1% " of noses, I'm sure. Thankfully, his previous owners, who knew nothing of keeping him fed, healthy, bug free, thriving and mentally sound, also did not know he had a first class tracking manner, interest and talent or they'd have undoubtedly sold him into the hard working life of government search and rescue. Instead, they were grateful their friend found one of my friends and I agreed to take him.

When Artemus came to me, he understood no words, he had no idea he could acquire useful information from humans and as mentioned, had not a bit of training. Left in a backyard and alone 95% of the time, this emaciated, kind, depressed giant made up his own stuff to do and a lot of that was squirrel chasing, ball chasing, anything chasing, really. And, why not? People didn't do much for him. He had loved them with all his heart and where had it gotten him?

So, I had no idea when I had a routine thought of leaving for a late afternoon hike one winter's day, that I was actually leaving for an adventure of the heart, a milestone experience that would measure a young relationship. No idea the most usual of habits would test three years of bonding, training and intelligence.

It was late afternoon and we were headed out in the 20 F degree weather for a walk. Late winter, I was simply delighted we had more daylight. I wanted to use every last bit of it. Famous last words, as my mother would say. So, I came back from the gym on a beautiful sunny day and headed over to the private road that runs through miles of woods and farmlands I know well, with the plan of heading into the state park. This particular park was founded by a Boston lawyer back in the horse and carriage days and it is riddled with bridle paths, cross country jumps, steeplechase fences and lovely expansive fields. Many of my young horses have learned and practiced their jumping skills on the variety of obstacles scattered through the miles of conservancy land.

One huge field lies way in the center of the park woods and trails spray out on both sides like twisting tentacles, usually enjoyed by a multitude of dogs and horses alike. Some lead up to other huge fields, others to more communal park areas for kids or bikes, but *tons* of trails and usually full of sounds of steel horse shoes striking the ground in rhythms I hear in my sleep. It's comforting. Solitude with the knowledge that somewhere others are cantering through or walking along on a loose rein, enjoying the same fellowship as I do with snow, forest and sky.

It is also true that escaping a paper bag has its challenges for me with my negligible sense of direction but my years of schooling and hacking in those fields were well spent. Gallops, training on the flat, fitness work, cross country schools and even, end of season tag on horseback with my students had laid an indelible blueprint in my mind.

I had also cross country skied in the winter if we were enjoying a storm, with two shepherds on my heels. They would amuse themselves by leaping onto my boards gliding under the snow and watching me fall, adding to the time I spent in the woods going nowhere. Like birds cackling with laugher, they would instantly high five themselves with a tooth clash or shoulder slam while they held each other's manes, rolling all over the snow in glee. I replenish there. I know no other woods where I would say the same.

Artemus, never much exposed to any terrain other than his backyard until he came to me, found everywhere we went a buffet of information. He's a natural trailing dog and he tracks his friends; not everyone, but his friends, nose on the tracks, until they are no more or I make him quit. The ideal candidate for a search and rescue team member. Nose to the ground, he'd rather wait to purge, wait to talk to me, wait for anything while he tracks his buddies or the latest quadruped of great interest, to pass him by. He also, in sounds of dead stillness, will lift his nose and snatch a scent right off the faintest air wave and be g-g-gone. Or, he used to, when we first met.

I also learned that when it comes to open space, Artemus "comes to play". Every day is game day. He accelerates to full gallop like a track thoroughbred, easily and for the joy of running. The boy has moves. He might eventually lower his nose for foot tracks but he resumes at the speed of light, still tracking. He's left me jaw slack, hands on my hips and eyes like tennis balls several times. What's there to say when he's already in the "spike" zone and out of sight?

In a blink, he is so low, his front legs stretching out at full capacity, haunches jack-rabbiting powerfully behind them, that he looks not unlike a jaguar. Emaciated and lame when he first came home, we worked hard at long, slow, restrained walks and controlled jumps straight up and down, not just to teach him manners, but to build up a slightly over-bred, severely underused hind end so he could carry the magnificent, long torso he bears. "What a fantastic job we've done!" I would think to myself sarcastically, watching him evaporate like a thought. "Well done!"

It's also probably worth explaining that Artemus Gordon, my little orphan-no-longer, is one of the largest German Shepherds I have ever seen. At a hundred and nine pounds of muscle and bone now, his head hits my hip bone when he sits and standing, I can casually drop my hand down to stroke him without tilting sideways at all. Blessed with looks that literally stop people in the street, he's also an exceptionally sensitive and kind fellow, contrary to the striking seriousness of his bearing.

A slave to his tracking nose, Hide and Go Seek, is his favorite game. Watching him work is like watching someone who reads Braille so fluidly you haven't yet noticed they are blind. He reads scent. Uttering only a soft "pssst" in the direction I'd have left him, I would hear him burst into a gallop, running my exact track, focused on finding me as fast as he can. In his head, I'm sure he doesn't even see his environment. He sees scent.

We play search games a lot since he's so talented at it naturally. As he gets closer to finding me, he carefully slows down, cantering loosely, calmly thinking, scenting. And then, he'll stop dead. I'm no more than ten feet away up a hill, behind a huge tree, trying not to breathe. He listens, backs up to my tracks, lowers his nose and walks right to me. His huge head lifts up sharply in a smile as he surges up to my shoulders, slaps a big kiss on my cheek and drops back down to circle my legs, long tail sweeping back and forth. He always looks at me with a clear, "Is this the best you got?" He gets a big body hug and whispers of how good and clever he is into his huge ears. I can't ever help smiling back at him in return.

Rarely, if ever, does Artie circle, showing signs of confusion or losing my trail. It can happen occasionally when I am sending him to "find" his football that I may have crossed tracks hiding in the house, but never when he is tracking me. I don't think he's ever circled even once looking for me.

So, it's a late winter's afternoon and Artie, now 3 years into our partnership, is healthy, fit, glossy and sassy, swinging along my favorite country road at my leg. Nothing on either side of us but estate properties owned by the same family, one daughter of which is a good friend of mine. Its peaceful gentleman's country, horse country and soul soothing.

Once past a half or 3/4's of a mile, there is another access into the state park from its backside off the dirt road. We've ridden from surrounding farms into the park this way all my riding life. It's usually horse or people access only, with its narrow winding paths. Artie is so excited to get past the white gate because it's rare the weather cooperates by being cold, no ticks, few if any horses or dogs jogging by to incite his shrieking which would put the Hounds of the Baskervilles to shame. So, winter rules in Artie's opinion.

He alternates trotting along straight ahead with flinging his head backward to stare at me, pausing anxiously to see if I'm coming and dropping his nose casually to smell which horses have gone by or anything else fun that he can find. We're in the state forest now and I call to him once. He spins his head, big smile and I hand signal him in, checking his concentration. I ask him to stop and sit a second.

I slide my hand over his head. "Perfect boy. Ears on, please." He hears me and goes to leap to his feet and I clear my throat. He swings back. I signal him to a sit again. " His active mind is perfectly reflected in his caramel eyes which he fixes intently on my face like, "yes, YES, HURRRY." I cock my head at him and pause another second to slow him. "Du calme, TT. Ears on" I repeat slowly, using his command language this time and I see him settle. He smiles, sits heavily, wags. I nod and release him.

Off we go. I've registered that I'm a little ambitious with the daylight left, but it was so nice to have extra time in the day, so we'll just go shorter and get back out to the road. Artie is playing with sticks, I'm hiking along letting my mind relax watching him play and return to my thigh with great branches and the occasional tree limb. We keep winding our way along, bursting into our first, second and third clearings, all perfect little oases in the woods, lined with stone walls, connecting jumps or banks and I fill his mind with jumping, "finding" and galloping after sticks I throw. He is BUSY....

I eye the two bottomless, muck-sided ponds for ice as we advance into the forest. The bank rims were white with snow and from the shallow, a thin coating of ice extended in about twenty feet to dissolve in a thirty-foot radius of unfrozen water, black and still. I mentally shy away from what I know my dog used to do - run like a wild thing for any scent and it could mean across water - and focus on my faith in him now to respond to me even in flight if my voice caught him fast enough. Besides, he hadn't bolted on me in forever. Onward we go, quietly throwing sticks, hand signaling, playing Hide and Go Seek. Two kids playing in a park lost in fun. Time to get back.

It was cold. Perfect for Artemus. I was dressed in yoga pants and warm, tall hiking boots, short down jacket, faux-fur hat and sheepskin gloves. Perfect for moving around, not as perfect for standing around, but who was going to be doing that?

It's amazing how you can just have a *fleeting* thought cross your mind and even as you try to eliminate it, you feel like you are two steps behind good sense. I forgot that dusk is feeding time for a lot of animals. Deer move, coyotes move, everything moves at dusk and early in the morning. It's cold. Scent holds in the cold. It holds best on wet snow, which thank God we didn't have but it was cold. I shiver.

All this starts percolating to me too late as I turn in time to see Artie fling his nose up in full tense alert, eyes fixed and push off into a gallop. He has dived into dense trees, weaving through deciduous trunks like he was in an Olympic level agility competition, nose fixed midway to the ground while I yell sharply twice. He doesn't even twitch... I stand frozen to the spot, eyes huge watching my mostly black, bear-sized dog disappear into thin air. What just happened? What is he..? Gone in 5 seconds. Just like that. I scan the woods and see nothing. "Ach.. Now, I have to wait for him. Naughty donkey," I think to myself, disgusted.

Two minutes - It could be a short one, I try to think positively. No biggie. He hasn't gone rogue in a LONG time. Relax. Wait. Give his mind a minute to settle, try calling again. I do it but only get more and more faint sounds crashing through the underbrush. I pierce the air twice with a whistle. Nothing. The wind has picked up. It is no longer nice. It's dusk. In the snap of a finger, the atmosphere has gone from The Enchanted Forest at Walt Disney to the colorless, branch-filled wood of the Hunger Games. I turn my back to the wind, berating myself for not having my longer parka on.

I pace around impatiently for a couple more minutes giving orienting calls to Artie once in a while. We're far off the dirt road in dense woods. "Well, you idiot. Well done me." I mutter quietly to myself. Shaking the encroaching thought that I won't be able to soon see in the dark, I pace another lap on my ten meter circle. It will take an hour at least, jogging the whole time to get back to the car and come back to the white gate with the horrible, weak little "emergency" plastic flashlight I have in the glove box. Why didn't I buy a big one when I thought of it? WHY? Three minutes gone. Nothing. Time - Start watching the time. Five minutes is the longest he's run. He'll be back.

I'm silent listening. The sun sets faster than you think and I breathe, reminding myself that he is strong and smart. He will use his head before doing anything silly I think hopefully, but knowing in the end, he is an extremely smart dog but he is a dog. A four-year-old in fur. With a super smelling nose that lures him all over the planet like a siren's song. I push my sleeve up to see my watch. He'll be back. The temperature is more like *freezing* degrees now. I strain to listen. If he's made the center field and crossed it, not good.... The park is ten miles long and about two wide. I pierce another whistle. Three sharp staccatos. I listen. Nothing. Three more. I flex my fingers in my sheepskin gloves and let the cold settle back around my hands. We had left the house two hours ago.

Five minutes. I start yelling his name and listening in the same rhythm of CPR. Silence. Wind. Cold. Bellow. Give him direction. Bellow. Silence. He'll come back for you, be calm. He's ok. Thoughts start to float more actively through my mind. I might call a friend in case we need horses.... I pat my pockets. No phone. Super. NOT good.. No phone. Forget it. No biggie. He's coming back. He'll be tired. He can wait here another 5 minutes with me to rest and then we'll make it out easily at least to the road before dark. Aside from the deer kicks, the coyotes and other threats to Artie that may lurk in the woods at dusk, I realize my main enemy is the dark. I will be useless in the dark.

I start to focus on the possibility that Artie is doing something I haven't seen before. And I'm not feeling him. I'm thinking ridiculous, useless things: trying to average speed and direction he went in, to a horse length of stride if I had one... and knew where to go... No. Try to find sunlight for direction.... Rises in whatever, sinks in whatever...No. He'll change direction a thousand times. Listen. Wait. Just a couple more minutes. Listen. It's OK. At least I know basically where we are. Just try to follow Artemus. No. Don't follow. He's way too fast. STAY. LISTEN. Be STILL. He is coming. I shuffle around in the field a bit, watching the outline of all the diverging paths getting softer and more obscure as daylight fades. I shiver again.

Ten Minutes...I start moving. New plan. "Get on a path so you can hear, closer toward the ponds, FOCUS. LISTEN..." My thoughts are jogging now again. I'm scanning and scanning. Nothing. A picture flashes in my head of 2 dogs being pulled out of the river that runs through many properties in our town ten winters ago, lifeless, having fallen through the ice. I wondered how their owners had not been with them? How could they not have known they were loose? "Well, now you know, don't you? Judging is bad. Right, just give me Artie back and I'll never do it again..." Wow, it's quiet in here. Not a sound. Eerie. Hell, the ponds.

I slam the picture right out of my mind. The wind is blowing now and the sky is grey and low and I hear nothing after every ' ARTEMUS, COME!" I throw into the air. Dead silence. Trees are creaking and cracking in the wind, but no hawks, birds, animals, nothing. My heart slowly starts to pound. Minutes are going by slowly. Slower than a hold up in a bank. This could be IT. He could be lost or gone. This might be the time. So, think. What are you going to do to find him? It's getting dark.

14 minutes. He has never been gone for this long. Waiting isn't working. He'll get lost if he comes back here and I'm gone. He'll be lost, cantering forever looking for me. Stop it. You are useless waiting. Waiting isn't working. The sun is setting. Waiting isn't working. Use your head. Mediate risk. What scares you most? What could hurt him most?

I breathe in deeply and slowly expel. 1) Water. frozen. Ice. He has no idea of ICE...2) Deer kick in the ribs leaving him helpless on the ground 3) Rabid coyote....4) He makes it to the road and isn't seen by someone driving by and gets....5) Someone catches him, he can't get back to me.. OK – That is enough of that list.

Stay cool. He's ok. WHERE the HELL is everybody? Not one person in these freezing, coyote-riddled woods on a cold, late Saturday afternoon of a long weekend in February at dusk? How odd. NOT.

If I move, he will never find me. He'll come here and I'll be gone. Calm down. He's so dark. He isn't fit enough to make the effort at that speed both ways, those people stole that from him. Those awful first owners stole his perfect health - CALM DOWN. I slow my accelerating mind with breathing. Calm down. Dread is growing as it does in people who have had a few bad things happen. We know it's possible. Horses die suddenly, dogs disappear, people you trust disappoint, choices must be made for good that will alter your future for bad.

Thinking of Artie not coming back was making it hard to breathe. I place my caring in places I can see. I see it in Artie. I had now been blessed with two of the most extraordinarily smart shepherds I have ever known and amongst all the numerous traits that made them so fantastic and so precious to me, freedom is in the top three. I have been able to make decisions based from strength all my adult life. I go anywhere and everywhere, confident with just my loyal, loving shadows loping at my leg. I live anywhere in the world and sleep easily with the most advanced warning systems ever manufactured. I didn't have a dog when I was five and lifted off the ground by my throat. A neighbor's mentally ill son at our lake house hadn't liked that I'd bumped into him around the curve of the wooded path to the dock.

This is just not good, but he'll be back. He'll find a way. Even in the dark. How will he know his way in the dark? I wail to myself silently. How will I know my own way? I feel my heart accelerate again and breathe deeply in and out, in and out. THINK. This is stupid. You are wasting time doing NOTHING. And time is what you don't have. Tic, toc. That and Artie. I shut the thought out of my mind as fast as it entered. Find a solution.

I stop pacing abruptly, body rigid. OMG you idiot, his nose. HIS NOSE!!! What do we do every day?" Some variation of "Find" his hidden football while he "holds" in another place" or Hide and go Seek. His nose!!! I feel a burst of hope fire right through my chest. He will know my trail. He will. He will follow it day or night and he will stay on it until he finds me. I know it. I don't have the type of dogs you have to always chase. I have the type who occasionally make mistakes but would rather be glued to me no matter how boring the activity. I have to get back to the road before dark. It's my only way to be in position to help him if something has happened. I need horses. Friends. Car. The gator! (Four-wheel vehicle), the Vet. Stop it. Get to the ponds.

High pitched baying. Two sharp screams, very faint. It's him. So far away it galvanizes me into motion. As fast as I hear it, it stops. "MOVE."

I turn and start running in the dull, faint light staying in a controlled jog as best I can. I trot out of my trail, back through the first clearing, then onto the rocky path again. I was a sprinter in high school. 3rd fastest runner in my province. Bad news? I cannot run distance to save my life. "Go slower. Breathe. Run like you're on the elliptical...Breathe...Long strides, even. Pace yourself...Wow, it's dark in here. Hard to see the footing."

"Ok, short strides, the footing is bad...Run faster for one minute, slower for two. He could be on the road by now. Ok - Run faster for two minutes, slower for one."

I want to thump myself on the head with a stick. I wasted 14 minutes by not remembering his training. What he's

good at. Forget him. Get to the water. I stop. Listen.
Call. Nothing. I pick up a run again. "He will track me. Don't
wait. Get to the ponds. Don't wait." In dead silence, the only
thing splitting the air is my voice, yelling north, south, east and
west when I stop to listen.

He never makes another noise.

'ARTIEEEEEEE.." "ARTEMUS, HERE!!!" "Artie,
HERE!!!" "ARTEMUS!" ... Nothing. I keep running. He has
never run and kept running. He has always been gone even
after deer for under 5 minutes. Then he was back. WHAT
happened?

Eighteen minutes... My mum made me comfortable in
the woods. Gave me a love of the woods. Always made them
seem secure for me. A safe place if you abided by rules. Can't
really say I was doing that currently. Deep in country, at dark,
alone, lost my dog, no phone. Rules. The bane of my existence.
Apparently, I forgot a few. Damn. She would NOT be pleased.

In my opinion, the only rule to remember is that no one
in their right mind wants to be in the woods in the dark. And I,
certainly did not want to be anywhere after dark without my
shepherd. I drag harsher and harsher air into my lungs. My
thighs prickle with the cold. Concentrate on keeping your heart
beats slow. Breathe. Keep running and focus on getting Artie
and not being alone in the dark without him. Stop. Listen.
Nothing. SLOW your heartbeat, breathe. Keep running. Do
stuff, don't think stuff...Where IS everybody? Not good. It's
getting darker by the second. Literally.

Of course, nothing bad will happen. You prepare
mentally to help him but nothing bad will happen. Just get to
the ponds. You need daylight to see the water hidden down the
steep slope as one pond is and buried in trees, as the other
is. Nothing will happen. Just get in a position to win. Don't sit
in the woods for bloody twelve minutes, waiting for a dog with
the best nose ever wished for by the DEA...
Nevermind. Bygones. Keep running...

I shake my head slightly, disgusted with myself. I swore
when I took this dog I'd not love him like Huck. He would

never be like Huck. He wouldn't. I'd never feel devastation again the likes of what almost killed me after Huck left. Mum was so sick.. Forget that. It's about Artemus. I was doing so well. Swore I wouldn't attach. Lovely on the outside, reserved on the inside. What the hell happened?

I know what happened. The dog just turned a corner one day. He started waking me every morning with a big cheek kiss. He started anticipating my arrival into the house. He started climbing on top of me to sleep when I was sick. He just started loving me like I was IT for him. He is cheerfully a cup half full kind of dog no matter what they did to him and one day, he just knew he was in his best life. So grateful for everything we do and what he eats and where he goes. And, the face. The face that barely registered any emotion for his first three months now expressed more in ten seconds than some men I know can in ten minutes. Dammit.

He's so happy to be included having been left alone almost entirely for the first three years of his life. He's a fast learner and he learns because he thinks the sun rises and sets on me. He just decided to trust me. He completely TRUSTS ME. And he could be in the pond, trying to swim, trying to hang on until...STOP IT. MOVE...So much work has gone into this dog. And, what does he do???? I'm panting and stumbling down a rocky part of a path. He blows out. Goes sideways. Acts like a dog. What was he thinking? He is in trouble.

I have to rest. I yank my jacket zipper open, panting and take my gloves off. "ARRRRTTTIIIEEEE!!!!" My voice sounds too light. No echoing sound but my own breathing. Keep moving. It's getting dark. Darker...Keep running.

I had been sure Artie would never be smart enough, close enough, funny enough to kill me like Huck. Just an arrow right through the heart and now, look at me, I thought, disgusted. Running with piles of winter clothing on, artificial joints, ready to fly off the top of that steep bluff into freezing water in knee-high, winter hiking boots if I have to, because it's ARTEMUS.

"STOP it," I pant to no one. "Nobody swims today... Keep running. If you worry about it, it will NOT happen. That's the LAW."

I finally stumble down the path between the ponds, hands on my knees, head hanging left and right as I drag air into my lungs and look for any disturbance in the ice. None. **Thirty-five minutes**.... That is a relief. First of the hour. He's not swimming. Damn dog.. I' m going to tie him up for a MONTH. I draw one good breath and turn my mouth skyward....

"ARTEMUS GORDON..." Pause. Nothing. "ARTIE, HERE!!!!" "ARTEMUS!!!!!!" It was the only frustrated thought I had had and in the echo of silence, it vanished. I stuffed my bad thoughts back into the recesses of my head. "Tell yourself a story," I mutter.

Better yet, get ON. I'm hesitating. My body doesn't want to leave this place. What if something happens here after I've passed. How long to dark? Minutes. My body wants me to wait here for him. It's practically dark. Still no noise. Silence but for the trees groaning and the wind. Come on, TT...Come on back, buddy. Come on, Artie. Hands on my hips, I pace. Pull yourself together. Be still in chaos...There are a hundred ways to skin a cat... Use your head. You must keep moving. It's the only way to help him in the dark. There was no time to wait. He had missed the window. Stick with the plan. Do NOT alter. He will track you. He will stay right where you go. Keep moving. It's not going to feel good but keep moving. Best nose grown on any shepherd ever. He loves you. He'll find you. Move.

What if he was kicked by a deer? Broken rib. Can't worry about it now. Nothing I can do. What if he isn't seen on the road, a stray car. Walk on the side when you get there. Move your scent to the side. I've got to run to Concord House. There's a phone in the new mare barn. I can call Louise. She'll get Jack, he'll get Susan, and so on.. We'll need horses. Flashlights. No moon. Keep running..It is DARK. NOT good.

I am running and stopping, jerkily. Running and stopping toward the dirt road. Up hills, over rubble and stones turned up in the dirt track, down hills with roots and more stones outlined in the deepest of shadows... It's pretty dark. My heart is beating in my ears and I'm sure it's beating way over 165...

"Try not to have a heart attack. Won't be helpful," I snap at myself. "Let's stay focused on being helpful." Breathe in for 3 strides, and out for 4... In for three and out for 4..Slow your heart…..Keep moving.

I look straight down not wanting to feed the apparitions that came to me behind every curve in the path, every tree large enough to hide a person, an interloper, an escaped guy from where was it again? Stop it!! I can't help the noise I'm making crashing and stumbling in almost full darkness and I push the pictures of things that would be attracted to noise in the woods at night from my head. Upside, it could deter all the huge coyotes we've seen over-running this park and keep them on the other side. Stop it. Your job is Artie. Look down. Watch your footing. Focus on the road. Get to the road.

I finally trot down the last steep slope and know the white gate is there. For a second, my mind registers that I'm out and about to be on the road, but when I last saw Artie, he was so far in.. he'll never find me.... Stop it. Keep moving. WHY didn't you remember your phone?

I have a moment, exhausted, when I feel my eyes watering from more than the wind. I've lost a lot of things in recent years. Artie is all I can't live without. This cannot be that day. A day of loss. A day of tragic accident. A picture of my Dad appears in my head and I'm remembering how he loved dogs. How he always helped me find homes for all the strays I would find at our country house or off the mountain in Montreal or on vacation somewhere. He always said animals found me. He also sometimes said it less with admiration and more with exasperation. He helped me place a lot of dogs. I'd always feel so bad when we had to leave the ones we'd rescued from the areas around our lake house with their new families. I loved them all so much at age 5 or 6, I'd be heartbroken. With my allergies, my parents were trying to not keep any at home. That, of course, couldn't last. I smile to myself in the dark feeling water cursing down my cheeks. Exhausted.

I hear my father's voice, clear as a bell, serious, willing me to understand, 'Sweetheart, what was our deal?" he'd say softly.

"No tears.....' I'd say, a big hitch in my whisper and eyes brimming with water...

"And why do we do all this work?"

"Cuz... they'll... be... ok.." sniffs and chin trembling.

"Yes, Sweet. They will be ok. I promise. They were lucky you found them and they will be OK. "

And I'd always whisper: " But I'm not ok..."

I shake the memory away. Artie is ok, too. Or will be.

I'm not happy. I've made the road. What if I shouldn't have moved. What if his nose is full with whatever he was chasing and he can't find my scent? I should have waited. Go forward. No time for backward. It's almost dead dark out.

'ARTIE!!" Nothing... "Artie," I whisper to myself. Come on, Shep.. Come ON. Hide and Go Seek, TT.. I will him with everything I have, to sense my upset, hear my calls, get on my wave length. Play ball, Artie. Feel the bond. The bond should have called him off whatever he was chasing ages ago. He is so rarely away from my side.

I walk a little way up the road each way, agitated, trying to beat back second thoughts. I call and I call. And then, I just stopped. Adrenalin starts retreating a bit after all the effort to keep my footing and my ankles from snapping on the trails. I'm tired.

45 minutes. He's lost. I am alone on a country road, a half hour's walk to my car in the complete blackness in one direction or a 30 minute walk into Concord House in complete blackness in the other. I needed a little minute.

I lean an arm against an old oak and hang my head. "He's ok. You'd feel him. It feels like hours. Forty-five minutes. It's fine. He's just a bad dog. How many years does it take, anyway? To feel nothing when things disappear? To 'be an adult" as a friend of mine would say, in private as well as public? I don't understand the concept even. Is being devoid of emotion adult? Being an adult means freedom to think for yourself. I see my caring in Artie every day. My horses and dogs see my caring, feel it and thrive on it. *Get used to disappointment*. Princess Bride. What if he is hurt or gone? You'll have to face it. Lock it up. BUT, let's find out first. Don't get worried just because it has never happened before. He's so smart...New stuff doesn't have to be bad. It's a different situation. Louise will ride out with you. No one is tougher than my friend, Louise. " I make myself laugh. For a half second.

And she also loves her dogs. This is going to be ok... My eyes are blurry and I shake myself to knock it off. If Louise was here, she would be tough as nails. Calm. Matter of fact. She would be going through all the same motions for her love of dogs, but probably not in the least afraid of the woods at dark. We'd be laughing. Making stupid jokes. Keeping our worry to ourselves. Well, I have that part right. Now, if I had a phone, I'd be spreading that worry hither and yon but ...Get on.

I push off where I have been silently blended into the shadows of my resting place and turn 180 degrees around to head for Louise's. I throw my eyes skyward and whisper, " Someone, SOMEONE watch for him on this road. He's so dark. WATCH for him. He'll be coming after me." Maybe Louise is feeding a little late today and she will be at her barn. (Louise is older than I am and doesn't look it hardly. Still fit and healthy, she competed and trained with us 20 years ago and has been a friend since I first came to this town. She has help to care for the horses on her farm but she still likes to feed herself, AM and PM.) If she wasn't feeding, I'd have to call over to her house three fields away on the other side of the farm. Thankfully, her phone number is one of the VERY few I remember from just forever, not lost in the forgotten abyss of disuse with the advent of smartphone speed-dial. My memory instantly loads the sound of her voice, reciting her number back on her outgoing message, with her exact lilting intonation and swift rhythm: "Hello, you've reached 555- ****. Please leave a message at the sound of the beep." The thought cheered me a bit. Not much, but a bit. Where is that damned dog. I wipe my cheeks.

Tired. Alone. In the dark. My mind instantly recaptured what I see in daylight of the way to Concord House with the same memory I use to walk cross country courses. Bends in the road, trees or scarcity of, the hidden drive that will be on my left at the third telephone pole from where I am, the bridge through the swamp that has a sharp dog-leg after it to the right, lined with small boulders, and then a soft bend left up a small rise in the road and I'd be at Baker's Cottage. Straight on another 20 yards or so to 4 corners lane crossing and left about 45 paces to the mare barn on my right. Phone low on the left under a shelf, once I open the door in the wing on the right. Fill your mind with DOING, not worrying.

Time to move. I take a deep breath and a last look up the incline behind the white gate. My heart starts to pound. I wasn't sure what I was seeing or if I should let it see me, but I had to. Please let it be... I straighten out of the shadows so I'm visible to sharper eyes than my own.

" Pssst" My heart is thundering in my chest. If it is Artie, he would know it's me from Hide and Go Seek. If it isn't, I doubted a wolf or coyote would come to me. I strain to hear footfalls, sure I am making him up with my blurry eyes.

A black silhouette still in the path, head hanging low moves silently, dragging himself into a slow canter with obvious effort. He moves not a rock, nor a brittle leaf making his way. It's either Artemus or a wolf. I shake my head trying to see. It's something black moving slow. Not helpful. It's cantering just like Artemus. Bigger than a coyote. I strain forward. A black head looks up, nose in the wind and drops again. He keeps coming down the slope.

OMYGOD. ARTIE? I can see his body is stressed by how slow the shadow is moving so I stay very calm, bracing myself for something awful if it is him and walk as quickly as I can toward the gate. The shadow doesn't hesitate but moves straight into me at a wobbly trot and falls dead weight onto my feet, panting, head hanging, looking up at me every so often but concentrating on himself, spent. ARTIE! I feel relief softening his body and I double over him running my hands from head to tail.

"Are you hurt? TT, omygod.. It's ok. It's Ok. Good job, Shep. It's ok. Where have you been?" I babble softly to him, frantically feeling his chest, running my hands over him. He looks up at me panting and moves his tail once. I feel my chest burst. Relief is starting to flow, heating my veins like lava in the evening cold. "I can't see anything. I have to get you home. Are you ok?? "

I'm running my hands all over, looking for punctures around his neck, legs, ribs, belly, the memory of his two baying shrieks in my ears... Again, he wags his tail once. I strain my eyes to see his face, checking for blood... He lifts his nose off the ground and kisses my cheek, then lets his head fall back on my feet, panting like a bellows.

I smile at him in the dark and allow myself to feel a little more relief. It wants to flood me like a broken dam, but we have Robert Frost's proverbial miles to go. The thought sobers me instantly and I stand upright.

"C'mon, we have to go. Can you stand, TT?" I say softly, praying he can move his 109-pound body on his own. "I'm afraid we have to keep moving. My beast rises and leans his whole weight on my thighs. I wrap my arms around him and hug him in the dark. I start to laugh softly. He wags his tail. Two swishes this time. We are in equal parts, relieved. I want to get hysterical because I'm exhausted, worried it's dark , he might yet be hurt, he needs the car, but I just gulp short breaths and hug him, supporting his giant head in the crook of one elbow, my arm through his front legs holding his chest up. Another solitary wag. We stay that way, me stroking his haunches to soothe his muscles and hugging him close again while I wait for him to straighten up and bear his weight himself.

It is now completely dark and with the adrenaline crash, I'm hugging my shepherd to rest him but also to gain heat. We were going to have to move. Artie's head, heavy on the crook of my elbow turns so he can poke me with his nose like he used to do when I first got him. In the middle of the night, he'd poke my cheek with his long snout to make sure I was there. I started to leave a nightlight on for him. I wish I had had one then. Whatever he had been doing, whatever herd of deer he followed, they clearly made him work hard. I slide my hand over his head still supporting his large, panting chest and am reminded that he is so spent, we're in the 'red' if I needed him for anything in the dark, in the woods, alone.

"Let's move if you can, TT," not a command but he still righted himself right away and followed me.

February is a desolate month. No foliage, winter freezing temperatures and daylight is a trick. You start to believe the end of winter is near. Spring and daylight advance but really you are weathering dangerous 'in-between' days. Icey ponds running under dangerously thin ice, trails that seem welcoming in the sunlight and are frozen, rubbled and ankle-breaking in the dark. Your heart seeks the anticipation of what great times lay ahead when you are actually rooted in what is yet unfinished.

He was too tired to even swivel his head up to look at me when I spoke quiet nonsense to him trying to soothe us both. I stroke his head and lean over to put my cheek against his. Tail swish. I had a brief laugh realizing how I chatter to open space when I am trying to keep my mind off things that bother me, and I was rattling along like a mechanical doll.

I thought of all the emergency situations where dogs, smart dogs, used to be the last call for finding lost humans, things, criminals and are now the first responders. And, how many people just don't like to be involved in an emergency situation. Less proactive, they rather keep "positive thought" and hope for the best. They have better tools too, for not caring if indeed, something really bad does happen. I was raised to do everything I can, everything I know, to right a ship. Today, we had both made it to the road and soon, we'd make it easily to the car, even in the pitch dark. Noone would ever even know what happened to us.

I understand too, why puppies like to be crated. What they want is cover, an area of safety of their own, which can be given without a crate, I might add, but I know crate fanatics who subscribe to them inflexibly and I have a sense of understanding now. Out in a huge expanse of forest in the dark, I hadn't been terribly comfortable myself, especially imagining my dog hurt somewhere with no way to find him. Being mindful and imagining a 'happy place' and other tools for subduing worry, wouldn't have yielded anything much today. Telling myself I could handle the situation, doing something to try, helped me think while I worried. I actually come from a family of worriers when I think about it, so I suppose I was fighting nature all around that day. Sometimes you have to work with what you've got.

A picture flies through my mind of my father on the deck at our ocean house at dawn, a historical tome he had waited all year to read on his lap, presciently knowing I would drive all night to get there when I had been asked not to, waiting for the nose of my car to appear in the drive. Worried. It taught me to respect those who do worry. He had been up at four in the morning, barely slept because I was driving. Why would I waste a beach day in the car? When he was dying in a hospital years later, I never slept. Every day I stayed awake, he stayed awake. When you worry about it, nothing happens. It's the law. It's my prayer.

I unnecessarily snap Artie's leash on about an hour too late and we carried on the long, very slow walk back to the car in the dark. Blessed quiet. Bolstered by the familiar strength of Artie's stride with mine, the dark was magically no longer a menace. We dragged ourselves along for another 30 minutes or more, stopping occasionally for TT to lie down briefly, which I let him do with a hand stroking his head to feel if he was alerting to anything. Finally, the car fob that I occasionally was clicking in my pocket, (almost every stride) registered and lit up the car like a spaceship in the inky black. It occurred to me that if stuff like this keeps happening, I'm going to have to rethink my lifelong affinity for black. Car, dog, clothes. Not helpful at night. Not helpful at all.

Artie knew where it was but I was happy to see the glow of the lights in the distance. We had skidded past what might have been a pivotal moment for us. Any one of a dozen things could have happened to him running blindly like that for MILES. I could have lost him. But he tracked me. God knows how far he had run. If I had stayed there, we'd have still been in the middle of dense woods in pitch black. We'd had a good scare but I did my job and he did his. In a blink we almost had a very bad story to tell all the people who love him, remark on how lovely he is or how much we look alike in winter (Black parka with my caramel hair and brown suede boots) or my neighbors who bemoan how their dog never swings along at their thigh looking so happy. I could have had to field all those polite questions I can barely take, the horrid questions: Where was he? When did it happen? "I'm so sorry" … Not enough time since the last loss. It's never enough time.

We reach the car and Artie eyed his new black hammock with his grey, thick travel bed in the back and did nothing. I help him place his forelegs on the step in and wait. He twists his head around to look at me like he does when he needs help. No jump. At all. I lift his hind end gently up, watching him army crawl with his forearms and then fold up like a deer and collapse on his bed.

I pressed the door lock for the first time I think ever on my home terrain, thinking a little preventative medicine was in order and start the car. I look over my shoulder at his face resting on a foreleg, eyes glued on me. Body spent, mind still alert. Thank God. He really was going to be ok.

"Your grandpa watched for you today. We won't be that careless anytime soon, again." The relief is real. Cauchemar! I finally let the hysteria loose and start to laugh. Hard. 'That has to be the absolute worst excuse for a lovely dog hike, I've ever had in my life. WHAT was that? A lower case Jon Krakauer? Into a Perfect Mess?" Still freaked out, I start the car, relieved tears rolling down my cheeks. And the methodology for controlling panic in an emergency needs tweaking. It is patently impossible to do anything in the dark with your eyes closed and wishing for a happy place unless you are Dorothy in the Wizard of Oz. The first rule of any emergency: Tell yourself you can do it. If you are not for yourself, then who?

My mum's winter rules that I no longer laugh at: (It just takes the ONE time) Driving long distance, refill at a quarter tank. Keep an extra jacket, boots and gloves in the car and sandbags in the trunk (maybe). Have a good flashlight. Never be close to darkness anywhere without Artie safely leashed and at my thigh. Be conscious of your surroundings. Don't blithely go off alone without a phone. Trust the training. Trust your assets. I'm sure there are more but I've a new one: When alone, don't be daft and forget the rules!

Not every victory is won on a scoreboard. Unbelievably, we won that day by a nose. Artie's nose. I look in the rearview mirror again at my shepherd, secure, serious and exhausted but seemingly alright. It had been a rattling afternoon when I had just been so happy about the longer daylight. If Artie had been even two minutes slower getting to the road, it would have launched us into Part Two of what would have been a hell experience, still ongoing. Just like missing by a nose in a horse race. Devastating for us. I could just as easily be tacking up horses in the dead of night with friends, trying to find him, instead of being warm and safe in our car.

If it had been another dog, lost in over a thousand acres of woods, I had no doubt I'd still be in the park. Those smell cells packed up and folded neatly into his lovely black snout proved themselves worth a kingdom today. More aptly, helped us out of our mess and back to the safety we always take for granted. My knees felt like someone had taken a hammer to them, my legs shook occasionally on their own and I had hot, firing pain up the ligaments on the outside of my ankles. Clearly, still not a long-distance runner and in fact, a lame, broken "never-again-runner", I still hadn't figured out how my heart had not burst flat open. Flashes came still, even securely locked in the car, of what we imagine can happen in the dark.

Artie will be happy to be home, curled into his huge, soft bed after a warm meal. As will I. I think we'll stay that way for quite some time. Time to give those hard-working smell cells a good, long rest. I put the car in gear and headed for home.

"The greatness of a nation can be measured by the way
its animals are treated."
-    *Mahatma Ghandi*

"Compassion for animals is intimately associated with
goodness of character and it may be confidently asserted that he
who is cruel to animals cannot be a good man."
-    *Arthur Schopenhauer*

CHAPTER FOUR

You Can't Make This Stuff Up

When I hear people talk about karma and the spiritual cause and effect of life, I'm not always sure I believe it. What goes around, comes around. Perhaps. A man turns into something good by good action and into something bad by bad action. Maybe. Seems to me though, that there is something more to achieving the spiritual heights of humanity or I'd have done a lot more philanthropy and skipped school. There are also large pieces of our society and culture who have suffered generationally and I'm not sure they'd say they've seen their oppressors duly corrected in any one of the recent decades.

Tutelage, however, comes in multiple-sized Trojan horses. Just when you have chosen an opinion or made up your mind about something, you are stunned by an avalanche of new facts that swarm you like soldiers at your mental gate. Those tiny fissures of thought which can crack a mind wide open to awareness, can gain traction just by considering what we don't know.

The idea of people who do bad things being evenly compensated in their next life is a nice thought but a roadmap with too long a timeline for my satisfaction. I'm more a "pistols at dawn" kind of person, I regret to say. I can wait patiently for the dueling appointment, but the length of my tolerance seems to be inversely affected by the size of the infraction. Short attention span, perhaps, (events in my lifetime is span enough I feel, to wait), but I like to watch, listen, learn and move on, in real time. It is just harder for me to retain memory of the insults I see and measure them against some activity eons away. I learned though, through Auggie, to pay more attention. Be more aware. In the end, I suppose it's a matter of faith.

I was not shopping for a new horse when I met Auggie. I would hope if you are shopping and you find a perfect match, it is the result of researching hard and long and making the right decisions. I wasn't searching, and in fact was a bit overwhelmed to have just accomplished my mission of moving to Boston for a job I thought I liked, with my lovely grey mare Gem in tow and not a friend in sight. I was hardly looking to add to my household or the size and complexity of an already large change in my life.

Massachusetts had been home to our family since I was born but not the area I found myself in for work and I had moments almost every day, when I felt I had pulled on a scratchy sweater and wondered how long I could stand it before I tore it over my head. Nevertheless, in a barn I didn't like, in a tiny town I didn't like, surrounded by a few tough people I didn't like, I met Auggie.

Anticipating all the joys of significantly better training in my sport of three-day eventing, excited to learn all great things, I found myself instead already embroiled in a huge battle with a barn owner, who but for the missing spots on her skin, resembled Cruella DeVille down to her nicotine stained finger tips. (She had cleverly been wearing gloves when we'd interviewed and generously refrained from smoking for the misspent twenty minutes I was there.) It had only been fourteen days but I had already absorbed the frustration of watching the same power struggle we watch daily in politics, reflected in the most common of situations. Wherever people believe their stature to have inflated past the people paying them, or offering them their friendship, or working for them, it doesn't take them long to explode into the all-out drama of the likes of Stephen King's Annie Wilkes, brandishing their crazy flags like rapiers. Misery, indeed. Sorrowfully, there was a stiff, enabling wind at that farm and every time I saw the owner, she appeared to me as Kathy Bates in Cruella's black and white fur stole.

I had kept my horse in a more rural situation too, before moving to Boston, so wasn't a fan of the Dickensian wheelbarrow feeding method they enjoyed. Probably filthy, (but we daren't ask) filled with grain of unknown origin, being pushed around at meal times, sweet Gem ate it but to be fair, she was really more a Labrador of horses than a picky, svelte Greyhound and certainly not a restaurant critic. I upped her flow of fresh fruit and veggies in compensation to make me feel better, but bad nutrition was not going to be sustainable long-term. Where I come from, we take stable management seriously and so before I had ever met or heard tales of Torrance Watkins' standards for barn care, I was a devotee. (You all know who you are.) None of the scenes I was living from Etables des Miserables, would ever be found in my own stables.

The proverbial straw came when I found Cruella beating a baby horse I liked, and suddenly all the task associated pressures of my huge move, settling into new housing, adjusting to a new job, having no one I knew nearby, all evaporated. I had to change barns. ASAP. And take the little horse with me.

I had run to the baby's trumpeting screams one night after work, racing around the side of the barn. Cruella held her and was telling her helper to hit her. My heart was already pounding through my chest when I skid to a stop, bracing myself like Wyatt Earp at the OK Corral. I hadn't met the owner of this horse yet, but I'd spent time watching her every night, in her dark stall, her back to humanity, slamming her foreleg repeatedly into the ground from shoulder height. Her head always hung, her neck showed signs of ring worm but when I could coax her to the front door, she had the most exquisitely beautiful face I'd ever seen. Her unhappiness was hard to bear.

When people ask you if you believe in love at first sight, I always think of those days, drawn to her stall, waiting for the moment she turned and came to me for the first time, huge liquid eyes timidly focused on my face. Connection. All that pumped through my veins as I skid around the side of the building. Everyone froze.

I love *The Princess Bride*. There isn't a section in it that can't be related to one of our own trials in real life. One of my favorite scenes is when the Prince, supposedly weak and incapacitated, stands and speaks with such gravitas and presence, commanding his rival to "drop…your…sword," that his foe, about to attack him, succumbs and in a one hundred eighty turn of bravado, drops… his… sword as he runs off. I watched Cruella's hand start to shake looking at me. My father used to plead with me from the time I was five years old, to try and manage the expressions flitting across my face. I'm slow to learn but somedays, I get lucky and my facial expressions are worth more than a thousand words.

Cruella spoke: "This isn't your business. Go back to your barn. This horse tried to kick me twice and she has no manners…" she was darting nervous looks at the baby mare with the beautiful face who wanted to kill her and I hoped she tried.

I retorted: "And neither do you. It is also very much my business. I've been asked to work with this horse and I'm about to buy her. Besides," my voice lowers and slows, "abuse in a place I pay board, is…for… certain… *my business."*

Thinking back on that moment, I recognized how much I had been missing a deservedly maligned, privacy stealing, big brother encroaching, internet application which would have been extremely useful in avoiding the whole debacle. I could have researched it on Yelp or Google or Bad Barns Are Us. The good old days. You just had to Helen Keller it.

Until the words flew out of my mouth, I hadn't realized they were all true. See something, say something. No one moved; the assistant, Cruella and I all stood glaring at each other. First, the assistant smartly dropped her dressage whip and ran off. With dramatic effect, I swiveled my head slowly to stare directly at her master. Ten more seconds and then, Cruella threw me the lead-line and bolted, saying something like, 'I'm going to tell my mother.' I remember thinking that explained a lot.

And just like that, the scratchy sweater came off. I threw my eyes skyward in a nod to my brother who had taught me, when we were traveling together and landed in a dodgy part of a big city that I was never to worry. Never be nervous. "If you act crazier than they are, they'll run! (I was a willowy teenager and in evening dress.) Be bigger and tougher. It's in the eyes. Acquire dead eyes, 'intense' face and master bravado. And when you're clear, get the hell away." And he showed me too, much to my horror, but it worked. (Do not run to a risky neighborhood and try this if you ever want to see your friends again.) The little group of threatening-looking young men disappeared however, and we leaped into the first cab we could find. Crisis averted.

I was mentally already in "get the hell away" mode. I'd commute to work. We were going to be happy "at home" before anything else. Now we just had to make it happen. The mare had stopped her hoof-staccato siren and stood. Sweaty, nostrils huge, she breathed in my scent, listening to me murmur to her, the alarm still not gone from her eyes. I dug around in my breeches pocket for a mint and cupped it in my palm. She definitely had ring worm all over her neck, some hidden under a stringy long, uneven, black mane. It was cold and I had gloves on, so I felt safe to pat her shoulder and breathe with her until we both calmed down. I also made a mental note to burn my jacket and gloves as soon as I left.

She eventually lowered her head and bumped me twice before letting her head drop heavily against my chest. I stroked her bowed neck behind her ears and waited for her to recover. It was a habit we would continue for all the remaining years of her life; if she was not feeling well or was upset, and even on the morning she left me, she had spent the night in the hospital with her head in my arms.

What was I going to do with a 2 year old?

'Hey, I'm Greg Collins...' the voice faded off watching us. "Oh, she's never quiet. As in, never. She must like you." He said quietly. Then added, "I heard you were my new trainer." His eyes started to roam over his horse and the look of masked distress on both our faces. Bravado is like a safety vest. Deployed one time only.

I stared at a man probably 20 years older than I was, calm, sympathetic eyes with a slow-moving demeanor and wondered how the hell he hadn't done anything to help his horse... And, how I was going to explain why I had interceded, taken control of something I didn't yet own and enraged the barn owners all in under ten minutes, which suddenly seemed like it might take some work.

I replied just as calmly, "Actually, I'd like to take this horse off your hands. Whatever you want for her."

He stared at us a minute, registered that I was still stiff with armor, that his horse was steaming and upset, and his small smile disappeared and gave way to a nod. "Wow, that is the worst business negotiation I've ever heard. Let's talk about it after we take Augusta back to her stall. What in hell happened here?"

Smoke poured out of Cruella's ears, her mother's ears and my own for the remainder of my week there, but it had the effect of blinding us all to each other's presence which worked out well. Like all disruptive change, good things were also about to happen. Sometimes, dead skin just needs to be shed. And, while I was ready to fight for Augusta, Greg knew he made the right decision to let her go.

When I was dressing the baby to leave a few days later in her new shipping boots, her safety WWII flying ace bumper hat and a smart, Tattersall stable sheet, she stood quietly while I babbled soothing noises into her beautifully cupped ears.

"This is your fault," I speak very quietly, locking eye to eye, "we are going to have to change your bedtime reading to *"How to make friends and influence people...""* Her nose slid onto my shoulder and her eyes were bright and happy. Amazing what a few days of anti-fungal scrub and antibiotic will do.

When Greg sold Auggie to me, I also learned our unhappy experience at Barn Bedlam hadn't been her first. Freely admitting his recently acquired curiosity about riding and horses, he admitted buying Auggie from a guy who was supposedly a good rider, but out of cash. Billy Preston. Billy was, apparently, often impatient with the foal but relentlessly banged the drum of her mother's athleticism, enough to get him more than he ought from Greg in Auggie's sale. Thinking he would be helping them both out, Greg bought the baby and dragged her with him and another older thoroughbred he had bought off the track for a song, hoping to learn how to ride. An astonishingly bad idea from a very good-natured man. And a flag. Any good horseman would have suggested better matches to his "friend" instead of taking a fair amount of money for a still growing baby from a man who knew nothing of horses. But, not Billy Preston.

Of course, those in glass houses mustn't pelt rocks and I had just bought an unvetted, snotty-nosed, ringworm-ridden baby when I did know better and wouldn't have the cash to add a more appropriate mount to my existing ménage if she didn't work out; Except, I did know she'd work out. I knew I had been put in that wretched place to find her and I really did know she would be great. If love can ever truly uplift anyone to the peak of heights, then she would be a champion.

We moved thirty miles away to a lovely town a stone's throw from the Atlantic, surrounded by gentleman's country, stone walls, fields and split-rail fencing. Horse heaven by anyone's standards and home to the best in US eventing. Stables were cleaner than some houses, horses ruled, paddocks were managed carefully and some of the best training and breeding facilities were spawning the country's winning show jumpers, eventers and dressage horses. If I had to go through that initial mess to get where I wanted to be with a new little mare, so be it.

Greg visited often. Through lunches and his visits to the much happier and healthier little mare, I came to find out that the 'great rider' who competed Auggie's mother, Billy Preston, was also connected to Greg in some friend fashion. Hence, he periodically spoke of him and his 'love' for Auggie. Apparently, I gotten the 'hell away' from one situation, but by owning Auggie, was dragging another around like Linus' dirt cloud in Peanuts. Every story he enlightened me with was actually a nail in Billy's coffin for me. So, I eventually ignored these ramblings of how well she was *not* treated, by a great rider I had never heard of, in a place no one serious had ever trained. It was hard to imagine what a small, barely two-year-old Thoroughbred could do to get into so much trouble. But, then, there is no accounting for people.

At least Auggie wasn't dealing with Greg trying to ride her anymore at barely two years old, thinking he was helping her out. "I thought I was giving her a little exercise," he said sincerely, while I stood expertly expressionless, doing my dad proud for a change, by not reacting. True, wild bucking and pronging from the minute he tried to get on, until his hundred-and-eighty-pound frame catapulted from the tack and bounced a few times, IS good exercise, for both of them, but not the most conventional training program if you hoped to sustain your interest in humble pursuits, like walking. He also informed me one day, that Cruella fell at her first spring event and broke a leg. Karma? Well deserved, rather. I felt if it had truly been karma, she'd have broken two.

Auggie was starting to recover, her coat became glossy and dappled, her mane and tail flowed off her in soft waves and her confidence began to build under the shield of her toughness. I bled inside if anyone said anything negative about her for the rest of her life, hugely protective of her, knowing how horrid her start had been, how sensitive she really was. I would never hear a bad word about her and deliberately wore blinkers better than any thoroughbred racehorse at Belmont. We were bonded and as tough as she could be, we also shared the same soft heart.

It became quickly apparent that most people in the area I had moved to, had coaches to select their new horses. I took a lot of flak for arriving in a fancy town with a large concentration of horsemen training to have careers in horse sports and towing a hugely magnetic, but naughty thoroughbred baby with me who, to be fair, had reason to act out. Some were quick to point fingers at my little wild child and scoff, suggesting she might not make the grade. At two. It didn't matter. I knew the second I saw her that she would be a great competitor. She wasn't meant to be a "spare" or a "practice horse", I knew she'd grow into a great partner. Time was on our side, the dueling appointment wouldn't be for years yet, when they'd see.

I made sure there were only good things and positive energy for the little baby. It had to have been hard for a decent man like Greg, who came to horses late in life, adored them but struggled to handle them with knowledge he didn't have, to do the right things. Selling Auggie to me was enough to make me forgive him.

Living so close to my horses and being surrounded by grass-filled paddocks, trails all around the town and hunt jumps dotting the countryside, was nirvana. All just thirty minutes out of the city. Auggie would hang her lovely neck outside her back dutch door and watch the sun set outside her 14x14 stall every night. It touched her. She'd be transfixed, just like any human watching the explosions of color at day's end settle into the gulley behind the barn. She might snatch mouthfuls and chomp happily, but usually she'd just sidle up beside me and watch the day give way in utter peace. As long as I was around and Gem was next door to her, she was dulcet. I gave her time to grow.

A little surprisingly, karma was being a real bitch to Greg. The misery Auggie endured with him wasn't done to her purposefully. He was completely ignorant of how to handle horses. In the end, he did after all, do all the right things by siding with me in that horrid place of a stable, selling Auggie to me and then staying my friend. And yet, she hated him.

He'd arrive so excited to see her and Auggie would try to kick or bite him for 6 months straight. He did things to deserve it, true, but learning takes time and Auggie had no patience for it. Cause. Effect. He'd startle her, she'd kick him. He'd try to stand beside her, she'd take her little hind end and plaster him to the stall wall for...minutes until I'd come running, suspicious of the sudden "quiet" in the barn. It was awful but she wasn't going to forget his association to bad times for quite a while, no matter how nice he tried to be. If he stayed out of her space, she nobly ignored him, if he even opened her stall door to say, 'Hi', she'd give a little side - eye before choosing her weapon-of-the-day from her protective arsenal and letting him have it. It was impressive watching her head work and not a little comical. But I felt that at some point, something good would have to happen to him if you believed in this life cycle of karma and true enough, a lot did. Just with other horses.

"Damn INGRATE!" he'd bellow after getting an unshod foot in the thigh and Auggie would blow herself up as big as possible, chest leaning on the lower part of her dutch door after chasing him out of her stall, fully confidant of my back up. There was full, flying mane accompaniment with her angry, head bobs, too. Insults were exchanged. Mr and Mrs Bicker-man at it again. Every. Single. Time. Poor guy. Kids!

And I would laugh. I tried to smother it, but a snort would erupt, quickly followed by exploding, nervous laughter. Not helpful. (Don't do as I do…) Some people just don't know how to walk away from a fight. Most of my first days in the new barn were mediating between Auggie with her new-found confidence and Greg; or Auggie and anyone who tried to manage her, other than me.

"I hate to say it, but she needs more time before she will be friends. Might be better if you are not in her space," I gently directed him, catching him helpfully, before he prepared to open her door one day and go in and greet Auggie again, whose eyes had squinted briefly before she calmly positioned herself to take him out if he made it past her threshold. I knew he'd hate my suggestion but better mad than dead, I say. My lips twisted and an eye closed, waiting for the explosion.

"What a pain in the ---! FINE." And he'd reluctantly turn his back and stomp off. Greg was learning how not winning could sometimes get him a lot further down the path to success than trying to overpower her. The lesson was not lost on me, either, in point of fact. Not to do with Auggie, who I had endless patience for, (clearly) but for people who sometimes were not particularly nice about potential they could not see with their myopic vision. Auggie was my heart's beat. As soon as her learning caught up with her athleticism and her very fast brain, there was going to be an unveiling. A reckoning. Whatever it took to get her to that point, was ok with me. I was merely the Queen's guard, and no one got past me to worry her. Ever.

It is an amazing thing and the gift of my life to be so passionate about horses, riding and the outdoors. It brought me a community of my best friends. Like-minded, intelligent, kind and uber-talented, I had finally found my place among them. There are bad seeds everywhere in life and the ones abusing animals or children are the worst, but they are thankfully the outliers. With a common bond of loving horses, I had tripped upon my own microcosm of being and watched, listened and learned about the good and bad in people, animals and life while my riding skills grew.

Where Gem was so inherently kind and easy to deal with, Auggie was building up an army of people who loved to take verbal jabs at me, knowing they had better be sweet and patient with her. I heard how some horses are just badly bred, that I spoiled her, that she'd amount to nothing if she didn't learn her lessons now. I would nod and smile and let it blow right over my head, in the same way I used to assess how badly a cross country course was riding by the level of horsemen who were having trouble. Always consider your audience.

I cannot explain why I had so much faith and love in that mare. She was everything I wanted in a competition horse and partner; funny, beautiful and brave; difficult too, but talented. I was giving her more time to settle in and she was calmer and more connected every day and even happily, slightly less dangerous.

There were days when her powerful will would be completely permissible to me, (I liked her to feel she was doing well) but there were also times when we had to negotiate. Augusta was a master negotiator. She didn't know it, but I did. And, it was the crux of our successful partnership. I learned how and when to ask or insist things of her, like most people learn crescendo, as part of concertos on the piano. There are times and places. Make sure they are important times.

After work on the ground until she was three, I started getting on my new little mare every other day. Just for twenty-minute walks. She would let me settle in the tack, just barely, and then buck down the driveway into the field. I could have snapped her head up, but I didn't have to. I'd slip my reins and mentally count off twenty seconds, then reel her back in and calmly set off for our hack, which I made sure was filled with doing things she loved. Seeing other horses, tooling around the neighborhood to get the occasional treat, ambling through the woods and feeding her mind with a little work. She understood calm. Eventually, she stopped bucking and walked happily off from the mounting block, chomping on a peppermint, head swinging, eyes looking for things of interest in the fields, realizing her habit of trying to buck Greg off the instant he tried to mount, was unnecessary now.

Eventually, we would only have a fit of bucks when she was startled. A deer. A hedgehog. A fox. Sometimes she bolted instead of bucking and on several days she did both, especially when a neighbor's four-in-hand team would come galloping at us over the hill in the field, carriage and footmen bouncing behind the thundering cart, moving like an audition for Wells Fargo Pony Express. The deafening cacophony of brass and harness clanging and banging literally made me fear for my life. Auggie would unhinge. There was nowhere to hide and to a baby, this was like trotting out of Central Park into Fifth Avenue traffic with a fire engine screaming by. Not good. I never had enough time to even throw a dirty look their way or I'd have been eating turf.

Not much about bringing Auggie on ever scared me, but that four - in - hand, driven by a world driving champion, who would no more care if you got launched into space than think one second of slowing her roll, routinely sent my blood pressure into unknown territory and left me trying to stick to my little rodeo queen like a cowboy's best eight second ride. There was only one horse I ever saw in my life, who *may* have moved faster running sideways for a full field than Auggie as a baby, but without the leisure to look at a stopwatch mid-flight, I wouldn't bet on him.

Those days when I had all I could do to stay on and try to keep Auggie steady when the death coach occasionally appeared to us, were some of the more acrobatic I have ever known. It allowed Auggie to practice and perfect her airs above ground, while I perfected being a centaur, neither of which I'd have committed to by choice. I prayed she'd stay sure-footed, crabbing at that speed across a bumpy field or if she didn't, that she would launch me straight at the driver of the rig. That would be karma.

More, I always knew I could never come off. N-E-V-E-R. I'd stick like a burr to her and quietly keep trying to calm her with my voice because I knew all my dreams for her were at risk if I came off. I loved Auggie madly, but I also knew she had a permanent little naughty gear just like some people do and if you let her unseat you, no matter the cause, she'd NEVER forget it and it would become her 'go-to' disobedience whenever you had a disagreement. But if you were firm and calm, stuck her airs-above-ground, her bucks, her skids left or right, she would eventually stop and carry on in a straight line, having packaged herself neatly through her wild athletic outburst, into a perfect galloping frame before she'd quietly downshift into an exhausted walk, like a baby's last hoorah before bed.

Sounds so much simpler than it was, but in the end, when I was coming back from a not-so-simple head injury, which was to occur a couple years later, the only horse I would ride was Auggie. People begged me not to, thinking she was too erratic. But I knew what they did not: she was incredibly sure-footed and had the prescience of a Pisces. Lighter than air. Secure. Intuitive. I knew she would never fall, never lose her footing and my worry getting back on after my crash, was that the horse would go down again, like he had in the accident. I hadn't come off; he had gone down. So, I rode my wild baby for the three months that "I could not sustain another fall" and she did nothing but exactly what I asked her, for all that time. No bucking, no antics, no nothing. A perfect lady. I had to be in company though, for the first couple months, and when my hacking partner at my barn had asked me for the fifth time, "Are you ok?" in an alarmed voice, I finally asked her why she kept inquiring.

"You are gasping every once in a while."

Yup. A bump, a tiny misstep trotting. Air would whistle loudly into my lungs. I hadn't noticed. So, I rode chewing my lip to keep my mouth closed. That had its own dangers, but I eventually graduated to making no noise as we revved back up to being fully healed and secure in the tack again. But, it was Auggie who did that for me. Gave me back the trust I gave her. Gave me confidence in myself again. It was I who needed the quiet consistency then and she gave it to me. No bucking, no excitement, she knew those days we couldn't fool around and she jumped up a level on her journey to becoming a mature adult horse. Was that karma? Perhaps. I call it love.

Greg remained interested in Auggie and flatteringly awed by her progress over the next couple years. He would regale me of stories of Auggie's early days still, (without any prompting), never thinking their content would continue to pit me against her previous owner, Preston, who seemed to me less consumed with horses than with making money off them. But, I tried to keep that confined to my inside voice.

We were at lunch one day, after visiting with the horses and Greg sighs, "Boy, Augusta sure is looking good! She looks just like her mother, you know, the horse Billy rode Preliminary all over." Big eye roll from me. "He always wanted to keep an eye on Auggie, hoping to buy her back when he could." I frown and my eyes narrow as I stop chewing and sit up in my chair. Wisely, Greg pivots to; "I couldn't believe how well she show jumped today..."

Like a terrier on a pant leg, I'm stuck at the word 'buy'. "You mean, the guy who beat her in-hand over a creek at a year and a half old to get her in from the field in Vermont? The guy who taught her to fight? That guy?" I scoff.

Greg laughs, "Don't be so hard on him."

"Don't be so enamored. I'm surprised at your choice in friends but no matter, you can put his fantasy life to bed, right now: The mare... is not... for sale, nor will she ever be." I say it slowly and quietly with Princess Bride gravitas.

Greg smartly takes a long pause. "He just always thought she'd be a great competitor... She is certainly tough enough."

I roll my eyes. Men! Tough enough? I was killing myself getting the "tough" OUT of Auggie. She was then four years old and was bigger, rounder, shinier and sassier than the sickly baby of yore. A picture of vibrant Thoroughbred athleticism and drop dead beautiful.

And, how she loved to jump! Work was play to her now and the thought of some heartless "moose" getting on her still-growing body and forcing her to listen all the time, when she was a bit of an arguer, made my teeth grind. Nope. Never. Hard No.

I smile with dead, shark eyes. "She wasn't born tough." She had piles of energy, true; was athletic and a pill; all true. She was also super affectionate, funny as all get out and crazy smart. She trusted me and she jumped like a BOSS. The end.

Greg, never one to pick up a subtle signal like the Rio Grande carved between my brows, carried right on: "Honestly, I think you'd like him. His wife is a friend of ours, too," referring to his own wife who I also liked. "I think they drink a little too much, but they love horses and he's really a good rider," he repeats again. I'm starting to simmer with insult.

I roll my eyes with a head shake this time. "Yes, the greatest rider I've never heard of. He could be Mark Todd and he wouldn't get this horse. Auggie will have one rider and you're looking at her. Her job is to be the best eventing partner we can be, not to be beaten into dollar bills. What a waste!"

"I think he just got a new job managing a farm out west. I think it will be good for him. He was released from a barn in Maryland, not sure why, but this new place will be good, I hope."

"The further west the better!" I say, suddenly quite cheered at the news.

Huge, dappled and sassy with confidence, Auggie loved her life. A thump or two of her foreleg on her stall door would bring her manservants running, (mostly me, worried she'd hurt herself - everyone else, knives out, yelling at her to stop), she was immaculately groomed and cared for every day, dressed in the best clothes, turned out for as long as she wanted and trained a little every day. Bossy pants, certainly, but like Tina Fey, more humorous, charming and talented all the time.

Auggie never had a cross country fault once she graduated from Novice, where she'd showcased her most memorable exploits. My only duty was to survive. Her attention was always dramatically on her surroundings, rather than her inconsequential fences. She just thought she was a one-name artist, like Madonna, gyrating to her own tune.

"Can I get you a different bit?" Friends in the warm-up would stand, eyes wide and wincing at the ridiculous reactions she'd have at competitors galloping past her as they ought or an official blowing a whistle, as they can. My jaw set in concentration, I'd shake my head and will my hips to stay glued to her tack. Just had to keep her on the ground and make it to countdown with her little rubber snaffle and a pound of "Saddle Tight" goop on each saddle flap. A huge, theatrical, side-stepping swoosh to the right or left, away from a horse, a fantastic capriole straight up in the air, a snapped buck on the way over a cross-rail or the all-time favorite, a pronging chip at the base of any of the first five cross country jumps, as if SHE HAD NEVER SEEN ANYTHING SO SCARY, jarring me a foot out of the tack before we'd reconnect over the fence. My friends were rightfully hysterical and would tease me incessantly, 'Ellie - Do the cartoon, up in the air, roadrunner face!!" I wanted to drink like an addict but then, of course, she'd have had me, so who had the leisure? I just prayed for the days when she'd have courses that grabbed her attention and I could keep my body parts. It was a challenge.

First events every season were like Christmas. You just never really knew which of her gifts she'd throw. In VA it was fence three, a tiny ditch and log and two strides out, still hot out of the box, she jammed her toes in, leaped up and zigged to the right, horrified by the tiny depression she suspected was a ditch. I just barely managed to straighten her on the half stride, zigging back to the left, in time to launch into the air to clear the obstacle. Auggie didn't just catch air, she'd make air 'Z's like a swashbuckling Zorro. Then, she'd gallop around like a champion the rest of the way. I'd still have no idea what happened, if it weren't for the video. She was that fast.

In MA, it was a pig pen and she wasn't sure she wanted to jump right in but she pretended she did. So, in a steady hand-gallop, without the smallest warning, she did her "dig and chip" routine, digging her toes in the last minute and pronging me out of the tack by a foot right in front of the trade show row and piles of spectators. Thankfully, she followed me into the combination but it's still my friends' favorite 'highlights' reel from her baby cross country days. And, mine. Her acrobatics didn't bother me terribly, but I saw horror on the faces of a lot of her peers. Nervous energy. She grew out of it, but Novice events with my lovely mare remain the scariest rides I've ever had.

In reward, came those blessed years of thundering neatly over any complex out cross country. The more complicated the better. She read lines between fences like she was ambling through Times Square reading the Bloomberg ticker. She'd amass the information like lightning and want to surge right in. Double banks into water, bounce Irish banks over ditches, trakehners, oxers, log mounds into black woods, drops to skinnies, she never missed. So brave. So talented. Such a great partner. We had our work cut out for us in Dressage at every event, but cross country and show jumping were hers.

Greg would usually come with his family to watch if a show was anywhere nearby, he was gaining knowledge and ability over time and loved riding more and more. Auggie's jumping just kept getting better and for everyone who had said she'd never be anything but trouble, I'm sure it was surprising to see the string of ribbons trouble could accumulate. More importantly, she rewarded good training decisions I had made mostly instinctively for her and my trust, by loving her job. When you can say 'yes', you should never say 'no'. She had a big will and a super mind. It was easy to make her days fun. It was imperative to make her days fun.

"Wow, she was great last weekend, huh?" Greg was having lunch with me after his lesson and reliving cross country from the weekend. "Billy asked about her this week."

My fork stops half-way to my mouth. We could go months without ever thinking of this guy and like thorns with roses, suddenly, Greg would bring him up. Not good.

Chomping into his sandwich, he continued without looking me in the eye. Always a bad sign.

"You know, he's back in Maryland and looking for another good horse."

"What happened in Montana? I thought he moved out there?" my eyes narrow.

"Not sure..." he stalled and looked at me.

I raised a brow not imagining what could have him haltingly deliver any news made for me. "And, what happened?" I prompt.

"Don't be mad," he started.

"Why would I be mad? He has nothing to do with me. What's up?" I wasn't mad, just slightly exhausted by hearing news of someone I really didn't care about and in my tender twenties, I really was a pistols-at-dawn kind of girl and if there were ever times that would incite that level of protective behavior from me, you could drop a dime in Vegas with the knowledge that it would have to do with my animals.

"I told him I'd ask. He made me promise, so I'm asking." Greg says innocently thinking his relationship with me was solid enough to sustain his constant blindness to my annoyance with this topic. But, it was starting not to be.

The hair on the back of my neck stood straight up.

"He's seen Auggie in the Chronicle when she does well and of course, he calls periodically because he's seen pictures..."

My eyes are going flat and black like a Great White's. I know this, because my friends tell me when I'm annoyed or when my insulin drops without lunch, that is exactly what happens. I was eating so, door number one. I allow my head to dip sideways and squint at him.

He laughs nervously. "Yeah, this is not going to go over well, but I promised."

"Anything you promise that guy should be secondary to what my friendship means to you."

"And it is..."

Big eye roll on my side. "Last time. Out with it.."

'He has a sponsor back in MD now and he wants to make an offer for ... her."

'Excuse me?' I do my utmost best to not leap off my chair but the top of my head feels like it may be coming off. When you harbor knowledge of someone who was responsible for deeply upsetting something you love, something you've had to put an incredible amount of love and support into just to make them come back to even, their very name grates on your nerves. I'm astounded and not a little annoyed that he even asked the question.

"I told him you'd never do it. He said to ask because he can pay you now. A lot," he adds quickly.

I was never one of the horsemen who came from never-ending, deep pockets, but I worked hard and got by. I achieved most things in my riding career on my own. I never did it expecting to make money flipping horses. It wasn't why I rode. You meet horses who will open up a lot of things to you, if you are paying attention, and they are the ones you keep. Selling Auggie would have betrayed my own soul and everything I had stood for with that mare. Knowing what someone thinks, being of like mind, intuiting their interpretations would make the insult even more sickening. Auggie and I were aligned in thought and trust. Turn her back to a horse abuser? I realized Greg didn't get it. Never would get it. Auggie wasn't chattel.

"Money?" I parrot stupidly. "Money for Auggie?" Beat of my heart, humorist and goddess extraordinaire? I think NOT.

"Mid five figures. You've really done a good job with her..."

I snort. "Ok. Here's the deal: I try to be polite because you know this guy who appears to be at best, an irresponsible man, a horse-trader with a track record of being thrown off every farm he goes to and let's call a spade, a spade: he abuses horses. He uses horses like hockey sticks by your accounting. I haven't seen a word about him or any horse he has ridden other than from you and what I have heard hasn't endeared him to me. I'd never sell her ever, let alone to that jerk, so please don't ask me again. You don't own her, I do. I'd sell myself on the street if I had to, before selling her. Not saying I'd rake in anywhere near the same amount of cash of course, but you get my point. Enough!" I scowl at him.

He belts out a laugh. I don't.

"Got it. I'm sorry. You're right. Thought I was being helpful. I won't bring it up again."

My jaw dangles open. "Helpful? I'm a little surprised having known me and Auggie for years now, that you haven't learned any better than to imagine I'd sell any animal to an abuser. Why would you?" I ask pointedly, still pissed off.

'I wouldn't. Sorry. He made me promise to ask and it seems a lot of cash. Just wanted to give you the option in case you hoped to move her on one day."

"Yup, I get it. And when Satan comes for you, speaking with forked tongue displayed, holding his trident and telling you he is Cary Grant, are you going to believe him, too? You've got the wrong end of the dog. AUGGIE, is who matters, not some long ago smoke and mirrors from a guy you really don't know very well. He sold her, you sold her. Enough. Do you actually think he rides better than I do? That she will do better with him?" I drop my fork again.

"Of course not!" Greg sputters wisely.

"Good answer. Then, again, you are connecting the wrong dots. Your job is done. We are stewards to horses; you, I, my friends, my coaches; Helpers not Users. Not back corner dealers. Thanks for thinking she'd make a windfall for me, but she already has, hasn't she? Given me purpose, excitement, joy and the feeling of success people need. What else is she expected to do?"

I purposefully look at my plate, re-direct the conversation and continue eating. "This Caesar is delicious..."

It was only a couple months after that lunch that I got a call from Greg in the stable during the middle of the day.

"I thought you'd be interested in some news. Got a second?"

"Sure, of course."

"Billy Preston died yesterday," Greg says slowly.

"He WHAT?" The guy was younger than Greg. More my age than his. "How did that happen?" I ask incredulously.

"He apparently went into the barn for night check a couple nights ago and decided to rug one of the horses. He walked into a stall and the horse kicked him to death. One double – barreled strike to his head."

I pause for a good beat trying to process what I heard. "I'm sorry to hear that."

"Yes, "Greg replied quietly. "Very sad he turned into such a troubled human being."

I was dumbstruck. I couldn't believe it. Saying even one word would have been ungenerous, so I let the silence hang and the obvious unsaid. You just can't make this stuff up. My eyes went skyward. Someone in the cosmos was looking out for the creatures and instantly made a believer out of me.

There it was. Out of nowhere. Karma. And, I didn't think she was a bitch at all.

"Seldom, very seldom, does complete truth belong to any human disclosure; seldom can it happen that something is not a little disguised or a little mistaken."
— *Jane Austen, Emma*

"Whoever said money can't buy you happiness, forgot about ponies."
--- adapted from *Gertrude Stein*.

CHAPTER FIVE

Be sure your sins will find you out....

When parents try to imbue their children with characteristics that will bloom out into their behavior later in life, responsibility is a popular one. How they choose to hop on that educational train is anyone's guess. Some have the time to ride that rail every day, some sit on it situationally, others approach it with a reservation for a "big talk" and still others waive at it as it speeds by. To a child, responsibility is a big word with who knows what for actual meaning.

Anyone talented at communications or marketing is already hot-wired in messaging and understand that "KYA" or Know Your Audience, is all that matters. My parents and my best friends' parents were no slouches. They "KTA" (Knew Their Audience). We, however, made their job easy. It's hard to hide impulse in those early years and when the only thing that brings you silence and time to work on your own for a second, is finding your kids playing with anything wearing fur, you've found a vein.

While none of the parents came from business backgrounds but rather professional ones, all of them knew they had been gifted with children who came out of the womb caring for something. Animals. And smartly, once that hook was in, they knew they could better explain or transfer 'responsibility' skills burgeoning in their offspring to other things like, say, the environment, stewardship at work, suffering, repeated tasks. Initially, I was sure "responsibility" meant rolling around on the floor with my puppy or bursting outdoors after school with him to gallop to the park. Briar rabbit to the briar patch. NO problem.

It's the nuance of responsibility that is sometime missed in early days and for some, all their lives. The thoughtfulness and discipline required everyday to make your own environment and all the stakeholders in its realm feel safe and cared for isn't acquired easily. Even the nicest children follow their id into hell when they are having a great time. Being thoughtful of someone else, not just yourself is something you try to layer like a cake into one's sense of right and wrong. If you are lucky, one of those layers will be same-minded friends to keep. If your children's friend-circle also includes ponies, 'partners-in-crime' is their layer. Not known for being helpful in doing the right thing, they are too infused with the same childlike sense of humor, playfulness and desire for excitement as their little human companions. Nannies they are not.

Sometimes, so enraptured with what you are doing, the extra step to avoid trouble seems a distant or wispy cloud on the horizon and not at all attached to the sunny weather pattern you stand in currently. Again, all of this becomes SO much easier to explain to a child when you have a lure. And a lure my parents had. I barely remember a negotiation in my youth that did not involve a merit system paid out in horse time.

As a child, your motivation for heading down one path or another can be complicated but my parents got lucky. Any behavioral changes about me were neatly fit into one of a couple boxes. Horses, (YAY); Ballet, (YAY), School, (yay); Piano, (hmm-I preferred my mother to play); Skiing, (YAY) Easily deciphered. So, while I also learned to hide things, be a little secretive, it wasn't because I was doing very bad things to myself or others, it was because even too much fun can be bad. Sometimes.

As I grew, I loved and rode Queeny in the summers, a 12 h.h. Shetland pony, who taught me the most important first lessons to riding without ever requiring an instructor. 1) When you are riding bareback and they drop and roll, wait until your heels feel the ground and simply step off. 2) The Thelwell mane, abundant and multi-directional, is your best friend; use it for ballast or keep your hands warm on a cold day. 3) If you hope to park your pony so you may mount off something like a hay bale or fallen trees in underbrush or rocks by the lake, make sure you have pockets of carrots and raisins, also good to share on impromptu picnics during your ride. 4) I hadn't seen Will Smith in *Hitch* yet, but I also learned to take antihistamines so my ears didn't curl up like cauliflowers, poisoned by green-head bites or my allergies, which ever got me first. It's all I needed to know. These were skills to keep as I spent a LOT of time on weekends all my youth, riding bareback all over the Green Mountains.

Little riders are said to feel their most authentic with ponies…It's a matching personality and size thing. If you burst out of the womb loving horses, interacting alongside a thousand pounds of muscle ranging three feet above your head with legs and hooves larger than one's entire being, it might make you change your mind about your mode of transportation. A more suitable partnering on your journey to athletic excellence, the poor house and a community of lovely, life-long friends usually always starts with something under 14.2 h.h. Ponies.

Every Friday night after school found my friend Beth and I in the barn, no matter the weather. Her mother always pleaded with us to wait until morning to visit the ponies, worried about what we'd concoct in the barn in the dark while she was prepping dinner, but she eventually got used to disappointment.

"Did you girls sit on the ponies in the barn again?" she'd ask, eyes narrowed while she set the table for dinner.

'Of course not!' my friend would say instantly, as we blasted into the kitchen, stinking of dirt and happy horses.

Her mum would shake her head. "You girls know you shouldn't do that. It's not safe."

While I was trying to figure out why it wasn't safe, Beth brazenly stuck to our story. "No, Mum. We just said 'Hi' and left."

"Ellie?" Her mother would smile at me, "I know you'll tell me the truth. Were you guys fooling around in the barn already?"

Visions of every Dutch, stall door hanging open in the barn, with hay strewn all over the center aisle came to mind. I gnawed my cheek trying not to burst into nervous giggles. It was almost like asking ducks if they had been swimming yet. It would have been unusual if we hadn't gone into the barn. This had to be a trick question. I lengthened my pause. It was habit that overrode thought, really. We would blitz out of the car when we got to the country, jam our bags in the house, stuff our pockets with carrots and race down the lane to the barn. My smile grows into a giggle. We had stuffed the ponies with treats, undressing their rugs and re-dressing them to groom them well, then climbed aboard our favorite two to brush their manes.

"Well, yes, Mrs. McGraw, we were in the barn..." I reply, hoping that was as far as it would get. My friend swallows a choked snort, that I thought only I could hear.

"And were you girls in the stalls?" Her mum asked.

"Um, yes, Mrs. McGraw.'

"Ellie, you wouldn't ride the ponies in the dark and without hats or me there, would you?"

I thought I better not mention we had not even a halter on them as we ambled up and down the short, pine board barn aisle, yakking about the week's gossip at school, lying down on their backs while they ate at the hay stacks along the way, staring at the starling nests in the rafters. Sans hardhats. Happy to snuggle with us, the ponies would amble calmly all over the wide-aisled barn, carefully carrying their young charges.

"Not in the dark. Nooo. We were just petting them and feeding treats.' The lights had been on.

She paused a breath to allow me to think I'd been clever and we'd skated through right before two eyebrows went north and a big sigh escaped her. She swung her glance back and forth between her daughter and me. "Well, I'm so pleased you both listened to reason this time."

We smile broadly at her in unison.

'Beth, darling, will you come here?" she said sweetly to her daughter. The minute Beth moved forward I sucked in my breath like I'd been tackled at a Thanksgiving football game.

'No, no, no, WAIT!" I spat out. Mrs. McGraw is bobbing her head now with a smug smile, in the timeless act of parents who are storming their way to a confrontational win. Racing their way to the 'AHA moment,' more like Agatha Christie than Oprah. Things were going sideways.

Beth swung her head around to scowl at me and then followed my eye line and grabbed the butt of her jeans as if her tiny thirteen-year-old hands would cover the huge tattoo of dust and horsehair there.

Mrs. McGraw grabbed her shoulders and spun her 180 degrees to look at the perfect horseshoe of red-bay pony hair on her daughter's rear end with feigned surprise.

"You'll be changing your jeans before sitting on any of my chairs, I presume?" Mrs. McGraw shook her head admonishingly a lot back in those days. 'Be sure your sins will find you out,' something my mum would say that took me a while to figure out.

Happily, we had parents who realized our misdemeanors were borne of a natural sense of adventure, fun, and animal fixation. They all also grew up playing in the woods as children and had seemingly turned out alright. They believed in children having a great time while incorporating a little learning of their own. So, what could possibly be better suited for us than being on a farm on the weekends? Nothing could, but it was a good thing the ponies couldn't speak, or we'd have been grounded by five o'clock every Friday night until Monday morning.

Parents also often tolerate the antics of their girls with horses mostly as a deterrent to them graduating to antics with boys. What our parents hadn't considered was the combination of the two, which became a fast track to watching chaos of the NASCAR kind.

I always make jokes about learning to volt at riding camp as a child and how it resembles the entire cast of Cirque du Soleil doing all their stunts on the back of one cantering horse, but I have used the skill of the 'galloping mount' more than Little Joe in *Bonanza*. Sometimes, it was in casual practice, other times, a pop-off at a jump when your mount didn't stop, or a quick one when turfed in the field, but the gold-medal-winning example of my expertise really shone like a beacon one early morning, when Beth and I had decided to take a hack, bareback, at the crack of dawn.

We loved Vermont and were blessed to roam it on horseback with the same appreciation that bicycles or a first car might mean to another. Freedom. Even better, freedom with friends, two and four legged. At just thirteen, we wandered rolling fields, hollows, thick birch and pine laden woods with panoramic views from every mountain rise. We had our favorite trails, knew every blade of grass, gopher hole and stream. We'd jump what we could find, walk where the ground was bad, let the ponies canter where it was good. Seemingly, an ordinary day for us on a Saturday morning in the fir-scented mountains.

During one of our incessant gab fests while in school, Beth had mentioned bumping into a cute farmer in the country store who had kindly asked about her dogs while she had waited at the meat counter to acquire some marrow bones. She squeaked out a "I wonder what farm he lives at? Holy cow, he was so cute!" rolling an adoring side eye over her shoulder for good measure.

"And OLD," I retorted, laughing, dismissing it from thought. Anyone out of school was "old" back then. That was all I remembered on the topic when time at recess was usually better spent talking of building jump courses instead. I should have known that the only bone that was never going to drop was that of where this farmer lived. The information had disappeared weeks ago into my mental Rolodex and there it sat until I realized on that early morning ride, after twenty minutes of what I thought was aimless ambling, we were still outbound from the farm and the conversation sprung from nowhere back into my head.

"Beth, what are we doing on the highway?" I ask trotting along the wide verge on the right.

"It's just a road, really. Not the highway. Besides, no one is up. We haven't seen a car and we just have to go past this big farm, past the next field and then a dirt road turns into the fields there. It's not far."

It was an answer, just not to my question. Beth would lie, cheat or steal if she thought the end result would be funny. Having spent years glued together in our love of animals, rescuing every conceivable type of creature in need, lollygagging over hill and dale on horseback and screaming with laughter until we cried, I wasn't one to question her motives. Suspicious, yes. Concerned, no. The two ponies we rode were hers. Beth was up on the cerebral, horsey-strided part Morgan, 14.3 h.h. bay named Justin and I was on a 13.2 h.h. Morgan pony called Maverick who could make an Aston Martin cry. If you EVER forgot to have a loop of mane in your fist when he burst into a gallop, it was an immediate back somersault into space with a belly slap landing and a long walk home. Because of that and other things, we called him Little Tricky or Tricks. Little Satan didn't have the same ring to it.

The two ridiculously cute bays with glossy round bellies, shocks of thick, black manes and happy, mischievous personalities enabled from the love of their young mistress, lived in the barn side by side and were turned out together too, like all good mates should be. Two weeks ago, Beth's father, who hid his large affection for the creatures under his gruff complaints, had begun regaling us at every lunch with a slightly suspicious lilt to his tone, of a seeming spike in fence repair he was enduring and which we both, naturally, ignored. In the days before CCTV (Close circuit television) a certain amount of expert skulking was required to solve seemingly innocuous issues like perfectly staunch split-rail fence snapping three or four times a week in different places on the farm, so her father took to indulging in a few more cigars with his scotch on their screened verandah over the weekends and was rewarded one day with the now familiar, ear-cracking sound of splintering wood. He carefully leaned forward in his chair, strained to see through the row of cedars in his way, to the action beyond. He watched, "Well, hell! That's not something you see everyday," he muttered and nodded his head in admiration. "Damn horses!"

That hadn't been long before our morning ride. Without the information, of course, we had no reason to be wary of bad behavior of any kind. Even our own. We were innocently ambling down a grass slope on the roadside to the valley below, coming up on a large farm with the house on the left side of the road and the cattle barn to our right. In front of the cattle barn, on our side, was a beautifully manicured, protectively fenced-in patch of green grass, bordered by petunias and begonias that beckoned to us like a mirage. Someone had even taken the time to mow it ever so nicely. But, in truth, it was the fence that sang to us.

Beth twisted around sideways and said, "We can take it like an in and out."

"No way." I stare across the road to the left. "There's a light on in the back of the house. The farmer must be up to milk his cows! He'll hear us."

"No, he won't, besides we'll be through before anyone even looks out a window and he isn't in the barn yet."

I eyed the pentagonal fence line with the pretty garden and guessed the rails were 3'3" in height but the strides across to the back rails, no matter the panel you chose, would be a crap shoot. Not that a bad distance used to bother us as thirteen-year-olds. The ponies usually sorted that out, bless them. It didn't look small from my bareback position on the shorter Maverick, but I thought it doable. The jump didn't bother me a bit. The freaky, early-morning-light-with-no-farmer in the cow barn yet, *that* bothered me.

I just knew he'd surely appear at the wrong time while we went about the business of trampling his lawn. When you love open space, you are quickly schooled about "footing". A farm with grass, crops and cattle stomping paddocks into mud but which maintains beautiful landscaping in front of their barn, generally means they had to work at it. They took pride in the property. With the attention deficit of youth, however, those thoughts never entered our heads so focused were we on jumping. The lawn was going to be the least of our worries.

I narrowed my eyes, "I'm not sure this is a good idea. We should just hack on by…" We were both jump mad and it took a lot for me to say the right thing, which was to say, 'no' since we searched the countryside routinely to find good jumps anywhere we went, but my gut was screaming at me to just slink on by.

"We can do it!" and the rest was lost on the airwaves behind Beth as she collected her beloved Justin and pressed him into a canter in the dusk of pre-dawn. Only, he didn't want to go. With all the encouragement that could be had from flapping elbows and determined Bean Boots, Beth and Justin were moving in an almost reverse gear, cantering on the spot, creeping forward to certain refusal. Justin and Maverick were best friends. Trix wasn't going to be a spectator. If Justin was on the move, so was he. I lunged for his mane just in time as he started throwing his weight from back to front in a growing hysterical staccato, trying to charge after his buddy. It was all I could do to hold him. His short, little back dodged this way and that under my seat like a Carnival ride gone wrong and I was already staring hard at the center of his Thelwell black mane, trying to stick with him. That short neck coupled with his tight little back could catapult Lucinda Green back to England from here, let alone me. 'Ricky, just hang on a second.. Trix! Whoa!"

All the while, Justin still hadn't taken the first part of the combo. I looked in horror at the turf under the rails and see less green and lots more dark brown trampled dirt. It was worse being the one to watch the unavoidable certainty of a wreck of some sort about to happen even while I was trying to not get launched onto one of our lunar outposts. He had refused three times now and Beth was losing steam. Swinging her head around to me, she hissed, "I need a stick!"

"Kick him. We don't have sticks." I hissed back. "We're stuck now." As ill-advised as this little exercise-gone-wrong was, we were now trapped. Justin had refused. All we knew back then was that he was going to HAVE to go over or he'd refuse all the time! Later on in my riding career, I became smart enough to know that sometimes, your horse is just trying to save a life. Justin wasn't stupid. Just us.

"I NEED ONE." A litany of words expressing the urgency of WHY we needed to make him jump...

"OK. I'll try..." Big eye roll from me since she hadn't even noticed my pony's agitation while she was determinedly demolishing a perfectly good piece of lawn. I scanned the ground further away for sturdy twigs, wanting to get all this over with before the farmer came out of his house to walk across to the cattle barn. Both horses were napping like monsters. Mine spinning in circles and leaps, hers not going forward and starting to whicker for Maverick. I saw a stick! No sooner had I slipped to the ground, somewhat of a kite to this little muscled race car, stretching for the branch, when a light *in the cattle barn* snapped open, immediately to our right.

Oh...my...GOD! We both hissed in unison, looks of panic and horror on our faces. Unfortunately, the horses didn't have the same reaction. If the Three Stooges could be Four, we'd be it. They were uninterested in slowing their bucking and spinning for a second, no matter how we asked and certainly weren't going to stop for a little 'light flicker', not grasping the finer details of what was about to happen to all of us, at dawn, on a stranger's property, destroying the only land that wasn't marred by huge cow pies and mud. Someone was up and already in the barn. I looked at Beth and with completely seriousness, said: "OK, we need to stop. Get off. We have to fix this."

Beth, in a full-on panic and way beyond the rational stage, yelled "NO WAY" and spun Justin around, kicking him with the strength of ten Gods now and charged him at the fence. My mouth snapped open in disbelief.

It was then, with the clarity of a checkmate moment, I saw that the ponies had a plan of their own. Too late. I saw it, I just couldn't fix it. We had a plan - to run, they had a plan - to be together. Justin clearly understood the urgency to move but was leaving no pony behind. Afterall, unbeknownst to us, every day for the past two weeks at their farm, Justin was jumping out of the four-foot fence line and snapping the top rail with his hind end to let Maverick tackle a much lower escape spot. So, Justin finally jumped into part A of the in-and- out to the ear shattering sound of cracking wood, AND... stopped. He didn't take the second rail and was now stuck in the middle of the pen. Churning up more turf. I was starting to be relieved that the sweat Maverick was generating, acting like a hopped-up rocking horse, was helping me stick better. Silver lining.

"Beth! Stop! Someone's in the window." I yelled, now with the jig up. Beth, in full-on hysterics, is weakening with every mild thump of her boots. Justin's attention was on Maverick and Maverick, only.

"Beth! Seriously. STOP!" Tricks was suddenly dragging us after Justin. The fence was broken and my mount and I processed that information very differently. My reaction was incomprehension. I may have been thirteen, but I had good manners on a bad day and some small sense of responsibility engrained.

Maverick, on the other hand, saw the fence and knew he was supposed to jump after Justin. I just never got that memo, so we were fighting each other like Wolfe and Montcalm in the French and Indian war, both very urgently executing opposite plans, the silhouettes of us like Stooges, banging into each other, craning around each other and lunging in opposite directions, etched again the pre-dawn sky. WHAT a show for the probable farmer/murderer guy, surely carrying a big ax, who was standing at the window of the cow barn just waiting for ridiculous little girls to come riding by. At our ages, drama came free.

While I was in my own battle, Beth was focused on one thing only - getting out of the pen. It was only Justin's decision to twist himself about in the small space and get a little half-stride runway that allowed her to succeed. She was crouched like a bug on his neck; Justin squats down and helicopters into the air and …Snaps his back legs out again, breaking another rail before landing and bolting for the road. My eyes skid to the window. Empty.

If my heart hadn't been young, I'd be dead. The door to the cow barn swings open and the outline of a tall guy in overalls is silhouetted in the doorway. My eyes started to grow like a "snapchat" dysmorphia until I could feel them max out, huge and round in my face. His were so tiny, narrowed as they were in temper, scanning back and forth from me to Beth, who was now yelling, "RUN, RUN!" as she galloped flat out down the side of the highway.

I'm... still... on... the... ground. Maverick is unhinged. I will say, to farmer/murderer's credit, he WAS handsome. Less murderous looking in person. Uh-oh. Hell. THE GUY from the country store. I'm too busy hanging on to a wild Maverick, still whirling and leaping, to be even more furious at Beth for running off. I stare however, at this Adonis in overalls, with the instant distraction of youth. Surprisingly, his reaction had changed from incredulity to disbelief at our stupidity. Maybe he wasn't so mad after all. Unlikely. I watched him stare after Beth, quirk one side of his mouth up in exasperation and shake his head.

In the dark grey of dawn, I still wasn't sure he wasn't a mad killer with an axe, but I was feeling a little better about it. I felt that he would have moved a lot faster if he was coming for me. Regardless, there are times in your life when you have to make split-second decisions that you know will have definite unappealing consequences later on. What I did know, was that I was too young to mediate this big a mess, so I just gave up. With his buddy disappearing like smoke down the road, Maverick was gyrating like an 800-pound cat in a bag. I locked eyes apologetically with the farmer who was NOT pleased at what he saw me thinking.

"Tricky" Maverick, sensed a turn of events and made a serious jailbreak attempt, ripping backward with the thrust of a 700 horsepower Superleggera sportscar engine. When I stumbled off my feet, he charged forward, banging me with his well-muscled shoulder on his way past me again to Justin. I wasn't letting go. It was muscle memory in the gap he created, to react as I had been taught for years at camp. I dug both my hands into his mane, regained my feet with two running strides as he galloped past me, jam my heels in hard ahead of his next near-side stride and let the momentum fling me up on his back. When I say the farmer was NOT pleased, at least he had contained himself. Until that moment.

We are cruising past the broken fence at Mach II when I heard a stream of hurled bad words not usually vocalized in front of young women. We were already on the verge of the highway, going about forty miles an hour so their effect was somewhat dimmed. That pony had gears. I wasn't about to fight with him anymore, I stayed as still as possible and prayed he'd be sure footed while he ate up the distance between us and Justin like Secretariat on the backstretch of the Kentucky Derby.

Kids always think they are so clever. Helps them innovate. If the worst happens and you end up getting away with it, it's not that abnormal to sigh a bellow of relief as we did, reunited on the lane which turned off the road into a huge field and where Maverick was already cantering on Justin's heels. Our relief and embarrassment were so great, we were hysterical, doubled over our horses' necks, gasping for air. Unbelievable. Prison-break about to be relived! Until a big, black pick-up truck pulled in behind not-so-Tricky and three in a row, we all burst into the field together. Not so funny.

Leaning out of his side window, he spoke very slowly for the temper I had witnessed not five minutes before, "Are you girls about done? Those horses need a rest."

We had far fewer gears than Maverick and that was it for me. Beth, thankfully stunned into motionless awe, recognizing her hero crush from the store, had pulled up beside me. Fully horrified at the whole mess, I leapt off Maverick and snatched her bridle in my other hand to prevent a re-occurrence. Beth had a very high threshold for shame or embarrassment. It wasn't out of the realm that she would take off again.

'I'm SORRY. We are SO Sorry. Really," I babbled while throwing a menacing side-eye to Beth. Beth just stared at the great looking farmer. SO much so, he looked at her, then at me and said, "Is she gonna be alright?"

My head snapped up to look at Beth. "Sure, of course. Yes, we're fine. It just was such a panic, the horses…" I gave Beth a full-on stink eye now, willing her to help me out. Nothing.

The farmer was now out of his truck, staring at Beth. "Aren't you the McGraw child? Two black and tan dogs?" Uh-Ohhhhh. I felt faint.

Beth bobbed her head, still speechless.

The farmer scowled at both of us. "I guess you didn't recognize me before you bolted off. Did you think that was a nice thing to do?" Farmer was still leaning out of his window like an aftershave model, only his face wasn't exuding his best possible "sexy pose". It was more a James Dean, undisguised look of patent disgust.

We both swiped our heads left and right like malfunctioning bobble dolls.

"Do you kids know what manners are? HOW could you break my fences and run off? In front of my face? Don't you think I work hard enough? Did you think I was perhaps blind and wouldn't recognize you? I don't get it. That was a nice garden my wife made there and you two wrecked it. Did you think about that?"

In truth, nope. But, we sure were thinking then. It was starting to percolate through our adrenalin-fused minds that this was an error that is going to cost us. AND not just cash. Could be ride time. This was bad.

I breathed deeply. "Sir, we're so sorry. I do not know what we were thinking. We never break fences when we jum..." I chewed off the rest of my sentence realizing it probably wasn't the response he was looking for.

Beth snorted and I continued, " I mean, we know it was wrong to jump at all but we didn't intend to create a mess like that and we will fix it. We'll come over and bring new rails."

Beth was nodding, still staring at him mutely like she was Lois Lane to his Superman. I was starting to worry that something really *was* wrong with her when out of the corner of her mouth, I heard, "We're dead." Phew. Hope stayed alive that I hadn't lost her completely.

A small tweak upward on the farmer's lip. "I think that is a good idea. You girls going to drag them over here on horseback?"

Hmmmm. Good question. 'No Sir, we'll find a way," I responded.

"I could just pick them up I suppose..."
That jumpstarted Beth out of her coma. The thought of having her Dad find out what we had done galvanized her into speech: " No, no, no... I mean, NO. We can do it. We'll bring them. I promise."

I bobbed my head in earnest agreement, still having no idea how we'd make that happen. Wrecking private property was one thing, stealing her Dad's car and trying to drive with rails sticking out the back window of his beloved BMW 5 series, at thirteen, would be quite another. Where normally we had no problem compounding chaos, the reality of our situation guided me back to sanity. Even we had our limits.

The farmer had opened his door and was standing against the nose of his truck, arms crossed. His head tipped sideways in consideration with narrow eyes and then he seemed to come to a decision.

"Alright. But I'd like you to tell your parents yourself, where you were and what happened. I'm not sure they would expect you two to be out here at six o'clock in the morning, racing your ponies into the dirt."

THAT hurt. Beth burst suddenly into tears and I flushed crimson with shame. Both of us reached out in reflex to stroke the necks of our horses who had only puffed for a minute before dropping their head to graze happily. Every ounce of adrenalin dripped out of our bodies and our heads hung. Truth be told since we hadn't really pressed to get to the farm, it was mostly just the Grand Prix sprint of the last 3 minutes that had taxed them, but we felt dishonored as horsewomen. We suddenly didn't feel very clever at all and could only imagine what this little interlude was going to cost us. Allowance was fine but riding time would not be. And, the horses had raced down the shoulders of a country road at dawn…This was BAD, also sometimes spelled: s-t-u-p-i-d.

'Yes, Sir, we will. We're very sorry.' we both said in unison.

"Alright then, you girls head home now and take care of your horses. You're lucky to have them." Kill shot. He gave us one last look and then ambled back to his truck and drove off down the lane…

When we were young, it always amazed me that adults, whether they knew you or not, knew exactly how to stick the knife in. Particularly if they didn't know you. Mentioning the ponies was just the worst. It stole our dignity and pride in ourselves as horsemen. We were ashamed of ourselves. As well we OUGHT.

Beth and I, who laughed in response to almost every single thing in our lives, stared at each other, mute, knowing the weight of a big lesson was starting to crawl around our shoulders. We mounted up and walked silently all the way home, groomed our horses until they glistened in the sunlight and fed them a delicious, super-sized breakfast and fresh water before beginning the slow, reluctant walk up the lane into the house. We argued all the way up hill.

"We can't tell Dad, he'll kill us."

"Oh, YES we can. Or the FARMER will kill us. We promised!"

"We'll never be allowed to ride off the property alone again. We can't."

"We have to and we're going to and we are NOT going to lie to that farmer one more time."

"He WAS cute, right?"

I swiveled my head around, feet from the kitchen door and finally, burst out laughing. But, it was short lived. The screen door swung open and there stood Mr. McGraw. "Girls! I was starting to worry. Breakfast is on. Where were you two?" He ran his eyes over us making sure we had all our limbs. I don't know how he had the courage to never worry about us, but he did. He trusted us. He enabled our adulthood because he thought we'd do the right things. Damn. The weight of trust was killing. Maturity through self-governance. This was going from bad to worse.

"I have a funny story to tell you about the horses. Wash up and sit down."

Beth cocked her head. "What do you mean, Daddy?" and we both bellied up to the kitchen sink. Beth shook her head vigorously in a 'Don't TELL him yet" motion."

Mr. McGraw was nonchalantly grabbing plates from the cupboard, about to serve. 'Girls, grab the juice in the fridge, will you?" He never looked up from the stove when he told us how he had finally caught the two horses in mid- fence-line-break and how very deliberately Justin cleared his forelegs over the rail and how he would make it easier for Maverick by dropping his hind legs through the rails and out would gallop Tricks after him. We feigned horror at the news naturally and participated in a lively discussion around finding a solution. We were going to hell. The size of the hand-basket was the only question.

We all sat down. "So!" a big pause and his face stills.

"Have you two ever seen the horses do that before?"

BE SURE your sins will find you out... It was all I could think. Over and over like the mantra of the damned. I didn't look at Beth. We were both silent. At thirteen, you are pretty sure your life is over when there is a big mess.

'Ellie?' he prompted.

"Um, I think so. Only once though." True. About two hours ago, I'm thinking. I stared at my eggs, shoveling them around my plate, not hungry. Nothing this messy ever happens without it dripping back to my parents, too. Aye.

"Beth?" he had dug into his eggs and sausage and was happily chomping mouthfuls, waiting for us.

Beth squeaked, 'I can't say that I have, Daddy. I mostly have heard them though." I swung my eyes to hers like she is mad before I realize of course, she would only have HEARD them as she is running off. Big eye roll from me.

He stared at us, wiped his mouth with a napkin and let us twist in the wind. "Oh, I almost forgot! I had an interesting phone call this morning." He stands to bring a plate over to the washer. "Yes! That nice fellow on Pond road - has a beautiful farm there, Jared. Jared Neil. You know him Beth. You've seen him in the store and he helps us out clearing trees when we need to." He was resting a hip against the sink, staring at us, arms crossed.

We whipped our heads to stare at each other in disgust. The farmer had lied to us! We were supposed to tell! I felt an empathetic pull for bass suddenly, running a line way out to sea, just before they are snagged. You think you've made it and BAM. Game over. Next time fishing, no running a line! Just hook'em fast, if such a thing were possible. Not as simple as he looked, our farmer, and way ahead of us.

Beth's father was nodding his head in that, "gotcha" way he must have mimicked from his wife. Beth lept to her feet and in a reversal of roles, I kept my lips sealed tight while she launched into what had happened with the rapid staccato of the best of Paso Fino hooves. He listened and then held up a hand. "Enough."

"Girls, I trusted you and I'm disappointed. I'm very happy your mother is in the city for the weekend and that we don't have to explain this to Ellie's parents who entrust ME with her care while you two are off careening around the countryside when I thought you up in bed asleep." Each word a dagger. His worry had never crossed our little minds either.

I clasped my lip between my teeth, slightly faint at the thought of anyone telling my parents. I'd have to repeat this discomfort all over again! My father was rigidly concerned about safety and drilled his children on it from the time they saw daylight coming out of the womb. He would not be pleased at our bad behavior and then at our disregard for telling people where or what we were doing, alone, careening around the countryside. Once he and my mother figured out that Beth and I basically drove four-legged race cars over hill and dale every weekend, alone, we may have been free-wheeling with our ponies but we would be pulled up short.

It's harder to stop someone riding when their horses were in their own barn. My parents could just choose to not let me attend my riding lessons. Mr. McGraw settled his gaze on my pale face.

"Worse though, girls, I'm disappointed in your riding abilities. If you are going to keep breaking fences, you'll have to stop jumping."

Our heads jerked up. A small smile carved his lips.

"I know you feel bad. Or, at least ONE of you do," he smiled at me and raised an eyebrow at beaming Beth.

"Regardless of that, there are going to be some changes around here and they start this afternoon."

We bobbed our heads in unison babbling apologies.

He held up his hand: "If you two ever lie to me, or withhold information again," his lawyer face on now as he stared hard at Beth, "There will be no more weekends on horseback together. Period. What you did today was irresponsible and dangerous. There will be no strike two. Got me? And, those horses love you. Don't you ever forget their safety comes first, as does, being a good neighbor."

"No, sir."

"Second, all jumping happens on this farm and NO...WHERE...ELSE. Are we clear?" a pause as I bobbed my head. 'Beth?' a dull roar.

'Yes!!! I swear." Her father rolled his eyes to the ceiling in certain disbelief. "Now, hop in the car. We have rails to pull and load in my truck and some landscaping to do. And by the way, Friday nights in the barn are out for four weekends which is the same duration you two will put in, if Ellie is kind enough to join us, at Jared's farm each Saturday and Sunday morning for two hours, fixing his wife's garden or any other chore he would like you to do. Rain or shine. Clear?"

Beth and I were suitably remorseful and grateful we could ride. We looked subdued and solemn with the realization of how many different ways our morning had gone wrong. Then it struck us, this was a bit like being thrown into the briar patch that briar rabbit had begged of his captors, because although thorny and a labyrinth to some, to him, it was ideal. Chores for Jared? Every weekend. Two hours a day? We swung our heads around to look at one another. The big, slow smile that came across Beth's face first, presented to her father as relief.

Later that afternoon, seated in fresh pine shavings in a stall in the barn, we relived the entire thing, moving about just enough to keep the supply going of more apples and carrots into the horses who sauntered in and out of the stalls to grab their treats, snuffle us for pats, nuzzle our cheeks and retreat to the paddock before dinner time. They were serenely happy and perfectly fatigued from all the excitement. How lucky we were. The horses were our best friends, we were best friends and we just existed through the week until life exploded for us on horseback Friday afternoons. You simply can't replicate the magic of being outside in the countryside astride a favorite horse or pony. The hijinks and the elixir were certainly high octane but our learning opportunities were too. Unlike a lesson you may or may not acquire from a book, these were teachings indelibly imprinted on us for life.

"When I bestride him, I soar, I am a hawk; he trots the air; the earth sings when he touches it; the basest horn of his hoof is more musical than the pipes of Hermes."
- *William Shakespeare*

CHAPTER SIX

Ledyard

When I finally moved to the little hamlet in New England where the US Three Day Eventing training facility resided, it was a huge exhale. It was there that the best on the east coast trained in Dressage, Cross country and Show Jumping in an equine triathlon made fashionable by the military back in the day. Woodstock to music, Boston to higher education, Cali to tech and Ledyard to eventing. A dream to a horse-crazy young girl.

Ledyard farm, owned by Helen and Neil Ayer, was where eventing really began in the United States. When what is now known as the Land Rover Kentucky 5 star held its inaugural show in '76, Neil Ayer had already hosted two of his three famed International Three-Day Events, the firsts of their kind in the USA. So determined was he to expose and educate American riders to the authentic level and expertise of eventing, that he paid travel expenses for international riders, most experts in the sport from the UK, to come to his events in '73, '75 and '77.

Princess Anne flew over and competed in '75. From 1970 through 1984, Jack LeGoff also moved from France to Massachusetts to coach the US three day eventing teams to an unprecedented eighteen medals in international competition including team and individual Olympic golds in Montreal ('76) and Los Angeles ('84); World Championship individual and team gold at Burghley ('74); and Pan AM team gold in Mexico City ('75). It was the heyday of the sport in the US and it was shortly after the Los Angeles Games that I moved to Massachusetts.

Neil was a tall, thin man with a luscious shock of white hair and a broad smile. He was one of our town's larger-than-life men from a different era. An era where entitlement was worn with charm and graciously put to the best uses for community, their naughtiness lauded as much as their successes admired. Their charisma was palpable and life seemed a bowl of cherries in their realm. If they hadn't been so inclusive in their enjoyment of sharing horses and equestrian endeavors with anyone who wanted to participate or so kind in offering their land and their egalitarian thoughtfulness to all hacking through or allowing schooling on their properties, eventing may have died on the vine for the very size of resources required to enable its establishment.

A true Brahmin, Neil was a gentleman farmer, sportsman, deeply wealthy, Harvard educated, sophisticated, dynamic, influential and above all, completely understated about it. He needed all those attributes and more, to bring eventing to a new level in the USA. His passion for the growth of horse sports and his unconditional love of horses was infectious but it was his egalitarian respect for everyone he encountered that signaled his disdain of snobbery or elitism and drew anyone with horsehair under their nails into his happy realm. He held all positions influential to growth in horse sports including President of the US Eventing association for years,

Master of Fox Hounds for the local hunt and an International course designer for two Olympics but was most passionate about educating people to higher levels of excellence in horse sport. On his own turf, a natural promoter, he added mystique too, to his events. His tales of the Boo-Golly Ghost on his farm charmed all attendees who made the trek to the haunted hollow which he had turned into a double drop through a gulley with log rails out at the crest of the hill. Not terribly scary but a pit of despair if not ridden well. Artful, creative and clever.

Neil invested in the pageantry, too, as bespoke great events. Splashes of beautiful color were everywhere in the organizer's beloved red and yellow hunt colors. On flowers, on the grounds, on footmen, tents, banners and jumps, they created a glamorous stage where everyone felt victorious just to be there, let alone ribbon. Galloping over the hallowed fields represented the best of tradition, continuity and accomplishment in sport and was a reminder of the equine ghosts of excellence past; the legendary spirits of Irish Cap, Bally Cor, Better and Better, Furtive, Victor Dakin, Marcus Aurelius and many more international stars leaving indelible memories on his farm. Ledyard became the only conceivable venue to select for filming the sequel to National Velvet in the US in '77 and Neil Ayer orchestrated that, too.

Neil made competition on his hallowed grounds your year's goal and always the most fun you'd ever had. A milestone for both horse and rider. More, if you handed him a beer and stopped to talk when you arrived, he'd generously offer up all the secrets to the questions that would be asked at every jump cross country! These elegant, gracious and visionary great men and women of sport and community crafted our sport and though I came to it in its latter years, they couldn't have endowed their generosity on a more grateful recipient or her peers. When you grow up horse-mad and finally make it to

Ledyard, it's like attending the Oscars as an actress. You only hope you don't fall on your face on the red carpet.

It was on one such Ledyard cross country morning, a year after I retired my upper level horse to illness, that I had decided to move my baby up another level. Auggie had had a great year, good momentum and I thought it best to let her move up a level while she was finding everything so simple and fun. Good strategy, good intentions, something about a road to hell…. Striking while the iron was hot, not adding all those miles back on her legs after her winter break was logical, only it was Ledyard, not the easiest of courses on any given day, but as a season finisher, was sure to be tough.

Every competitor readies themselves differently for cross country. I always worried about bringing my horses home safely and to that end, tried to remember every blade of grass on the course, every ride for every stride, so I was quiet in the pre-performance zone most times. In a ritual as old as gladiators readying themselves for a spectacle, I moved quietly to get her cross country gear on. Cross country is never something you want to engage in with anything but a calm mind in either you or your horse. It is the jockey's duty and obligation to bring his partner home safely, just as it is theirs to jump technically correctly. Auggie's eye was serious and I was filled with worry and concern that this might not be the right event to move her up. She was so brave this wild thing I bought as an almost two-year-old. Her mind could whir at the speed of light, too, but I'd put in almost three years reversing the frequency of her bad memories. None the less, moving her up to preliminary at Ledyard was feeling like a mistake today. Some fences still weren't sitting well with me after three course walks. I tried hard to shake the bad feeling off.

Auggie nipped my arm as I was about to lean over and place another protective boot on her foreleg. I smiled at her and stroked her forehead with a full palm. She blinked, stopped shifting on the cross ties and dipped her head a second, leaning her weight onto my arm, a habit she developed early with me. She loved a head hug and when she wanted to let me know she wasn't feeling well, or that she was connected to me or that she was happy to see me, she dropped her lovely head on my chest. I tugged her ears, smoothed her neck and placed her tack on. No one spoke in the barn but everyone could hear the speakers blaring a mile away through the woods.

My last thought always, when I leave stabling at home or away at an event to hack to the start, is how privileged I am to have two fabulous horses to ride and train with, how I have loved the sound and feeling of hooves in a strong gallop and the blank pause as we are flying over natural obstacles, almost since I can remember. How much I am in awe of horses, their majesty, their intelligence, their talent. How much fun cross country is. It focuses me on doing the very best I can every time.

I studied Auggie's face earnestly, watching how alert but calm she was, and it took me a little by surprise. It was hard to not have a Rolodex of her baby mischief scrolling in my mind so I almost missed the maturity that morning, missed her confidence, missed her whole new countenance lately on cross country where she kept paying the first-string-horse- chit she'd been asking me to give her. It was hard to not think of her as my brave but sensitive baby compared to Blue's good humor and sophisticated polish. I have no doubt she knew Blue was sick and knew she was now first string. She'd wanted it a long time.

Blue was, indeed, home. One of the first horses in the Northeast to contract Equine Protozoa Myelitis and live, thanks to the supreme efforts of the Cornell Veterinary Hospital in Ithaca, New York, he was now throwing himself around his waist–high banked stall, as I hacked away from him on his tempestuous younger sibling. He, too, wasn't used to having Auggie be first string. Our charge up the levels and my chance to confirm him as a solid Intermediate horse finished with the onslaught of his terrible disease. It was heartbreaking to me. Not just because my trajectory upward would now be arrested, but because I loved him so much. When Blue galloped and jumped it was literally like being on the wings of eagles. The air was amazing. He made me look good on the flat and I started to acquire a taste for exerting myself in dressage because of him. He was rarely, if ever, out of the ribbons at any level. We were very close. This sport is unforgiving though, and we would learn a lot about disappointment and other life lessons, on its back.

That Ledyard morning, I left the stables with Blue screaming at me, the sounds of his anger following us half way through the wooded trails on our way to the event site. I rubbed Auggie's withers and neck again, steeling myself to his calls.

Traveling everywhere with Blue and I as she had for two years, Auggie was always happily rowdy. A wild child, she'd amuse herself with all sorts of antics anytime she had audience. Often heard banging stall doors for instant discussions about her lack of carrots, raisins or her man-servant (me), she would also perform like a starlet, caprioling through the air whenever she would go for her first walk around any new show grounds, jigging here and there, Madame Melodrama. It was always like escorting the female version of Ozzie Osbourne; fabulous, but a handful and a little dangerous! That morning, I had gone through my whole ritual and realized, she was deep down serious, deep down calm and as I threw a leg over the tack and quietly walked off with her, I wasn't quite sure what horse I had under me. My hand soothed her wither again, as we continued down the long drive. You work for years to make a great cross country horse, a great eventer and then when she shows herself, I almost missed the signs. One day does not a professional sport horse make people will say. I would say, somedays, one day really DOES a professional sport horse make.

I cannot say the number of times I heard someone say dismissively to Auggie's face, as she grew and I so clearly adored her, "Pretty is as pretty does!" or "That mare has a huge attitude. You shouldn't spoil her," like one training method worked for all. What is true about success is that how you treat those around you matters. I never saw Augg as anything but a sharp witted, talented, loving mare and we reap what we sow sometimes. Horses are individuals just like humans. Auggie needed a lot of rope in order to trust and perform like a star the days she was asked to, but some horsemen feel they have to control and modify the life out of sunrise. I'm sure there is a horse for that, but it definitely wasn't mine.

So, this particular event morning it was hard to imagine Auggie had given up shenanigans for Lent or even Ledyard, no matter how she had grown the last couple years. After all, she was still just a five-year-old. We hacked further along the driveway planted on both sides with walls of rhododendron, flowers gone by, their rubbery leaves waiting for next spring to release new exquisite balls of fuchsia. I was running the course through in my head.

One of the worst fences for me to get comfortable with was surprisingly not the famous coffin at Ledyard. I had a very bouncy, short-backed mare who made me comfortable show jumping by her carefulness. Slowing her would be the question there. Having raised her with respect for her confidence, it would be a question of when to start slowing down, when to package her and still keep her speed rolling, how much throttle to cut. I know that ride. The one I didn't like was the huge trakhener in the field ¾ of the way around the course. It was a 14-foot-wide irrigation ditch with a massive log suspended over it diagonally. No ground line. A Ledyard legend and a big confidence question before you landed and made your way to the second and larger water complex, I felt doubt waft over me again about moving up a level for Auggie at an end of season competition when the jumps are normally larger for their division and this event being in our backyard, just made it more difficult. All eyes would be on the hometown riders. It was like walking a red carpet with a monkey on your back.

My coach and friend, Brooke, was transitioning herself into the sport of Dressage and was attending a CDI (Concours Dressage International) in North Carolina herself, and not in Massachusetts at all. There were some of my team of friends who hated competing without her. I, for the most part, was always fine. I had grown up going to competitions on my own and was well used to coping, but today was different and I had friends to help but was missing her. It is in those moments that I really grasp the brilliance and innovation of technology. The telephone was a spectacularly game changing invention and my appreciation of it couldn't have been more than on that weekend, when on the night before cross country, after the course walk for the riders, my phone rang.

"Ellie?" Brooke's voice boomed into my kitchen, "how is it?" she asked.

'It's a little bigger and more championship-like than I would prefer for Auggie's first prelim."

"I've heard that from a couple people," she replied. "Well, it *is* the end of season, we knew it wasn't the best time to move her up, but her momentum is excellent right now and you believe in her."

"Yes, I do. I just never want to hurt her making a mistake."

"What's bothering you?"

"The trakehner ditch in the roadside field. I've walked it 4 times. I just can't get comfortable. What if we deviate slightly from our line and she can't make the width with that huge log? She's not Blue Boy, she likes to get in closer to big jumps. What if she doesn't see the takeoff, there's no ground line for her, and slips right into the….."

"Ellie!" Brooke interrupted. And here it came. The benefit of us all living and training on every bit of grass in our town. She didn't need to be here. She knew exactly what I was talking about and had ridden it herself several times. "That is not going to happen. Auggie will see the ditch and here's what you are going to do. You have a spot on the road for you to line up with?"

'Yes.'

'Great. You are going to land from the vertical in the field before and let her breathe a couple strides. Connect her gallop and when you turn her onto your line, turn your toes East and West and F-I-N-D a ventricle. When you land, you can take your heels off her…And DON'T wear those ridiculous button spurs…Wear the soft tipped longer ones so you don't yank your legs out of position trying to get your heel on her."

Brooke liked to paint a picture for her students of exactly what she meant and occasionally she "overdid" for effect. I'm still stuck on the "ventricle" part of the conversation when she says, 'Ellie! Hear me? Get on that line, keep your eye on your spot on the road, don't run her off her feet, keep her connected and you GO. She will absolutely know the ditch is there."

Suddenly, I had clarity. I smiled into the phone. "Ok. Thanks."

"You will be great. Call me, eh? When you are home. Call me. Don't rush her at anything, remember her ride. Call me…."

As Augg and I hacked along through the woods, I was visualizing my ride to every single fence. I went over the instructions for the ditch and moved onto the water and then the oxer uphill. Auggie and I were through the hunt club grounds now, the loudspeaker blaring louder and louder as we got closer. On a long rein, she swung along loosely, her pretty ears pricked. I rubbed a hand over her neck.

We soon bumped into another friend who trained with us, who was also heading over to cross country. Neither of us was happy about all the alarming 'holds' we could hear coming from the announcer. It wasn't a great feeling. We were about to cross onto the property when we saw a splash of very bright teal leap the paddock fence line two fields away and start its approach to the ditch and hanging log. Exactly the fence I was worried about. Jessica and I stopped and waited. It was a Canadian rider, flamboyant in the brightest blue riding colors and on a jet black horse headed to the ditch going way too fast, or in Brooke's terms, "riding her horse off its feet". Jessica and I looked at each other. "Do we look away? I don't want to have this ride in my head..."

I grinned the smile of the dead. "I know, but I don't think we have much of a choice at this point. Holy COW, she is going way too fast." We stared, fixed on the approach, wincing and trying to settle our fit horses who were sidestepping and dancing nervously while we asked them to wait.

One important thing about horses. If you ever think of disrespecting their intelligence or forgetting their input as part of the team sport you do, they have a nifty way of reminding you. The black horse was gunning down the field with her ears pinned to her head. The rider was flapping her elbows and leaning forward, in the perfect 'hell bent' position, which is a deadly sin. I remember my face contorting in horror and my eyes narrowing.

"Uh-oh, " Jess and I said in unison.

In a second, on that beautifully green field with split rail fencing dotting the landscape and century old trees swaying in the breeze, this small, black bullet slammed her brakes on. She skidded so hard, her front legs slipped past the edge of the ditch, launching her neck over the hanging log and flipping her rider neatly up and over the rail in a full, spectacular somersault before she dropped into the ditch five feet below. Jump judges appeared instantly to help her horse back to terra firma and again, the announcer's voice boomed across the field, "We've got a hold at fence 28. Hold at fence 28". Super. The ride of my nightmares.

Talking over each other, Jessica and I said in unison: "Totally pilot error. Nothing to do with us. Rider blew it." We nodded trying to reassure ourselves. We shoved the thought away that the course was not seeming to ride brilliantly that morning.

The rider crawled up out of the ditch then and I looked at Jess. "Ok, let's go. No more spectating for me this morning." We smiled grimly and walked across the road onto the property and headed for the warm-up.

"Do you think we should wait and see a good one go?' Jess asked worriedly.

"Oh, no. Nope. I don't. I think we shake that off and get to the warm-up." I didn't want to say out loud that I had a bad feeling we might have to wait too long for a "good one". It wasn't a fence I wanted to study. I had a plan and I was sticking to it. I tried to erase the image of the teal and black body in full extension going up and over the tree trunk to land in the ditch and how she had crawled out covered in mud with her helmet tipped sideways over one eye. She was going to need a new hat cover. Bet she thought that was worth the trip from Canada. Not good.

Thankfully, I had a great friend in town that weekend. He was an extraordinary rider, a US Equestrian Team competitor and used to live at my house when he was in the northeast for the summer. He'd keep his horses in my stables, we would take jaunts together up to different courses in our area for cross country schools with our young ones. One of the funniest people I know, howling laughter was our hallmark. Not that I anticipated we'd see any of that before we finished cross country today, but he was a comfort to see to be sure, with Brooke away.

Talented, intelligent with a gift of riding seen only in the top riders in the country, he could ride a flying pig, get it home safely and then have it bring him a beer, he was that charming. My mare adored him. He had never ridden her but he played with her every day in the barn. I relaxed as soon as I saw him waiting for me in the warm-up.

"Auggie girl!!!" Augusta instantly lifted her head and made a bee line for him, so Teddy could pat her, making both of us laugh.

"Wow, so the Canadian..." Eyes huge, I was shaking my head left and right.

"Yup, heard that one from here. Forget about it. You know you have options here. I'm never one to advocate a pull but riders we know, good riders, trained riders, are falling at the coffin. It's riding not as well as we'd like for a baby,' he stroked Kate's face again.

"Yup, " I said tightly. "I know."

"Hold on course, Fence 23." bellowed the speakers... We looked at each other. "There will be an hour delay while we wait for one of the ambulances to get back to the property. Regulation necessitates we have at least one here at all times. Sorry, ladies and gentlemen, you will get a fifteen minute warning of the course resuming, as soon as we know something."

Great. Both emergency transports were clearly on their way to the hospital.

"Apparently a few other fences aren't riding well either," he joked.

I said with a smile, "I think I have a plan. The coffin comes after the big Irish stone wall and is parallel to the finish line. Exactly at the end of the first loop and before you start the second going out over the coffin. There is one of every type of obstacle in the first loop, including that huge bounce bank and a small trakehner. If she feels worried, if she is losing confidence at all, I'll ride to the finish instead of the coffin. She won't know she's being pulled off, she'll just think it's short and we'll just be done."

"Good plan." Ted said. I could tell just from that, he was worried. There was no follow up joke. No laughter. No teasing. Riders don't generally ever think of how to NOT go. You always are committed to go. You had to be. But I'd also rarely if ever heard the amount of mayhem going on as what was happening on course this morning. It was hugely unusual. Unusual times called for unusual compromise.

"She will be fine." I walked off around the warmup to diffuse the energy building up in me. Stay positive, visualize perfection, stay relaxed for Auggie. An HOUR. Dear God.

I remembered Auggie's first competition at Ledyard just a year ago. She had gone novice and my parents had flown in to watch both her and Blue go around the prelim course. Auggie had flown around the course like a star until the small water near the end. She hated water as a baby and right as we approach, I caught site of my parents, always a little concerned for me doing this sport anyway, parked under a huge oak tree.

I'm gunning Auggie's engine a bit and didn't trust her not to refuse if I slowed, which was a mistake. She got mad and right at the lip of the water, dove to the right, rose up on her hind legs and ran sideways for four steps with me curled forward like a burr on her neck and before I could get her down again.

She wasn't even particularly upset, she just wanted me to know I had "pushed" her too fast and she wasn't having any of it. Super. I circled at a more regular speed, calmed down and re-presented. In she went. There's no pushing around a 1200 pound animal. I made a bad choice to ride the approach in a way I never trained her at and she let me have it. I petted her in apology, as we galloped away, both of us trying to shake the refusal off and my parents' wide-eyed expression of horror.

Some days you go to train, some days you go to win. And that had been just a novice water jump. I had to remember that lesson staring down a field to a fourteen-foot gaping ditch today with a 3'7" fat log staring me in the face. I felt I owed that Canadian a 'thanks' for the reminder of how not to lose your discipline on course. I sent a little prayer skyward that I wouldn't be reminding someone else of the same lesson, very shortly.

Horses were running again and Auggie was concentrating and moving well through her warm up. Ted waved me over. "Ok, so Julie just galloped down to the steeplechase fence completely out of control, had a runout and came off," he said matter-of-factly. "You know, we can always live to ride another day. It's a little crazy out there today.' He wasn't laughing.

We were all pretty talented riders with good coaches and horses. We worked at it. We loved our horses too, and this sport, but you couldn't help knowing bad things happened to people just like us and the day was not going well. It was a high risk sport made less so by as much education as you could get. What grounded me though, was how much I loved the feeling of running and jumping and ergo, so did my horses. That was what I had to think about. Cross country is what I did better than either of the other two disciplines. Sometimes you have to bet on yourself in a real and material way. That was one of those times.

I took in a deep breath, quietly listening to how responsive Auggie was with every soft squeeze of my fingers or rub of my calf on her side. She was ready. I looked at Ted and smiled tightly, "I like my plan. I am going to start."
He nodded and moved right on, off that grey area where succumbing to the slow, billowing nerves rising up like a fog, seems very inviting. "You need to ride the terrain here. A lot of up and down and bending lines and speed changes. Check your

engine all the time and stay compressed all the way with her.
Go slow. We're not here to win today. We're here to compete
and teach her. Go slow. Keep energy in the tank all the way." I
nod silently, fully concentrating on the course now, ready to go.
"And Ellie,' Ted looks at me as I am riding a small circle in
front of him, "any bad jump and get off the course. It's just not
riding well today."
"Yup. I will."

In my head, I'm gearing up past my nerves, past the
pictures and sounds of a bad eventing day which we rarely get,
to the calm focus I need to feel my horse. It is my job to smother
nerves in order to make good, fast decisions out there for her
and give her my best ride. I trusted her and she me. We were
going to be fine. A lot of being good at cross country comes
from loving it, which I did. I loved running and jumping and on
days like that day, I suddenly realized that is what I usually am
thinking about in warm up! Not moving up a level, not being at
Ledyard in front of everyone in town, not how badly the course
was riding. Just of Auggie and how we love to run and jump.
We move closer to the start box.

"60 seconds, number 103." I nod, lean forward to tug
Auggie's ear and stroke her neck as we walk around the start
box. I can feel my teeth clamped tight and I force myself to
breathe. "From fifteen seconds only please," I ask our starter,
not wanting to have Auggie unhinge at the box listening to them
count every five seconds from thirty. She jigs a step or two and
then settles back down to an alert walk.

"30…." Auggie caprioles straight up into the air as she
always does, shocking everyone around us but me. I am
perfectly still and with her as she lands and jigs. The timer
stares at me, mouth agape. "Sorry."

I shorten my reins. "10…." I move Auggie into the box
and keep her ears pricked out the back.

"5…4…3…2…1…Have a good ride!"

"Thank you." I turn slowly, take two trotting strides out of the box before accelerating smoothly into a rhythmic gallop to the first going away fence of fat logs in a big brush. I hover my seat over the tack for two beats and close my calf. Auggie steps up her stride a bit and leaves the ground, easily soaring through the air and landing in full gallop into my bridged reins.

My first concern for her was fence three coming up very fast. It was a trekhener over a ditch, smaller than the one at the end of the course, but horses were refusing. It was too early in the rhythm of the course and you needed a solid campaigner and a good ride to make light of it. Auggie had had a training issue at this jump when she was a baby. It was just a ditch at the time, no log, but she hadn't liked it then and she had a really good memory.

Fence two, the rock cradle. Very square, set a little after a downhill and in a grove of trees. It was wide and Augg blows over it like its nothing. I'm pretty serious already about making sure she understands today is NOT a day to have conversations about approaches and who is driving. I needed her to listen to me and instantly. So far, so good.

We land and I still worry her mind isn't wrapped around a knife blade like mine was. It's fence three. The small trakehner. I close my leg and feel her surge correctly into the bridle, packaging her momentum but still worried, I scrub my bat on her shoulder once to tell her it's important. I gallop strongly ahead in not much room in the grove, break my line, sit in behind her wither with my eye fixed on the rail above the ditch. I wasn't a fan of trakehners either, truth be known. Auggie bolts in retaliation, then settles two strides out but she is furious that I even placed the bat on her shoulder. We're away like it was a joke except that I'm suddenly in a major battle with her now, arrogant on the best of days and now, wildly unamused with me. The crop rub was an insult and I was paying for it. I was riding her as a baby in transition and she was mad. I had taken her excellent concentration and completely disrupted it. I was over-riding out of worry for her and she had already been perfectly on the job. *Nerves.*

We were careening down a hill that slopes away on your left toward a huge stone wall coop and Auggie's ears are closed. People we know from all over are in town and out and about on course, certainly catching us careening downhill, out of control. Super. Not my best display of her talent this season but I have other thoughts to think, like how I'm going to get her back before the jump into the small water. She shakes her head when I try to close my fingers on the rein and is thundering too fast, down the hill. We take the sloped stone wall like Sherman through Atlanta and carry on down the hill to the first water, arguing all the way. Not good. I can't get her back and we're moving way too fast. There is a vertical set one stride in front of the complex and we disagree all the way up to it. It's the same water taken in the opposite direction as when she had almost run my parents down a year before. I shake the thought off as quickly as it came.

I am sitting as still as possible when she leaves the ground a stride away from the vertical. Not good. I slip my reins and stick like a burr while she slams her legs up into her chest, lands on the grass before the water's edge, twisting a little to clear the vertical and then launching herself into the water without taking the stride that was there. We're galloping out before I know what's happening. I take a swipe at shortening my reins. Wisely, she knew she'd startled herself too, not just me. She lets up on the gas and we re-connect and move forward, glad to be alive. The course really began for both of us at that moment. We shook the nerves off and began to ride.

It wasn't unusual for Auggie to have a lot of energy in the first half of a course. Today, though, I was responsible for it and very lucky neither of us got into trouble. She was back to concentrating on the flags ahead. I deliberately stay at a slow show jump canter as we turn and line up to a jump built in between two trees. It's narrow. No place for an error on the line. My lovely mare takes her first deep breath on the course, canters in perfectly and threads the hole between the tree trunks. I let her surge forward to effortlessly bounce up three big, bank steps and gallop away like a practiced campaigner. The coffin is two jumps away.

After the water fiasco, I began to realize that Auggie was jumping incredibly well, even with my riding errors. The only thing she had questioned so far on this course was me. I had been over-riding her. Over-protective. I felt the trust that was inherent with my big french horse transfer seamlessly to my young thoroughbred. The crowds, the size and complexity of the jumps weren't registering to her. I stopped thinking about protecting her and started to ride the course with my partner.

I held our pace, got off my horse's mouth and guided her shoulders onto the line of the big Irish bank. There was a ditch in front, which she would see up closer and she would need to jump enough to cover it and land, put in a very short stride and leave the ground again off the back of the bank, which also had a ditch on the landing side. She'd need some motor, but not enough to force her back into the air too soon. I was going to have to let her choose. It was a bit of an awkward distance on the crown of the bank, too. Blue always bounced it. He was bigger and longer and didn't mind standing off a big jump, he had that much spring. Auggie needed to touch the ground, I was sure. I *wanted* her to touch the ground and stick in a short stride before the backside effort. I hear Teddy in my head reminding me to go slow, keep gas in the tank…

Auggie blows over the ditch, landing on the bank with her forelegs and instantly pulls them back up to leap off. My heart stops. It's too wide with the landing ditch. I slipped my reins to follow her full neck extension. She was going for it. Not the slightest hesitation. She blew on and off so fast, no landing stride at all, a perfect bounce and we were gone. So far, I'd been a step behind her the entire way and she was taking me to school. My mare, in an instant, made it very clear to me that nothing was going to bother her. She was riding the lines and cruising on to the next set of flags. I just needed to give her the right speeds and presentation and stay out of her way. The training was there and the new size of jumps at this level, wasn't backing her off in the least. I recovered from falling a little behind her like a pony-clubber and gathered up my reins as we galloped along to the tower oxer where we would have a perfect, explosive jump, clearing the oxer by a solid foot and turning right to the coffin.

I hear the announcer for the first time on course, 'And a huge jump over the tower stone wall for number 103 and Augusta. They are clear there and headed to the coffin..."

People are everywhere. Crowds left and right and beyond. For an instant, it's all I can see, then Auggie's on the line. She has let me shorten her stride and is bobbing a little against my hand, wanting to keep her speed on the downhill approach. This was not a place to indulge her or be tired. I remind myself that unlike Blue, whose size demands that I begin to package him very early for technical combinations, Auggie's forte is carrying speed in closer, being packaged fast and reading the combination like a ticker tape before she executes precisely. Today, though, we go slow here. It's now or never as to the left of the coffin, further down the field was the finish line. If we were going to pull out, now would be the time.

I felt everything that I cherished about my brave mare, flow through me. I sat lightly down on her back, hugged her sides with my legs and held her, hands in front of me, elbows quiet, keeping her on her line. The coffin had been sending good riders for ambulance rides all morning. My eye fixes on the top of the vertical, slats leaning at us which they shouldn't do. Auggie is three strides out and locked on. This is one time I don't want her to get close. All the other horses were getting in too close and getting their knees under the fence. I lower my hands, soften my fingers and she springs forward to hit the early distance I wanted like she read my mind. I keep a feel of her in the air as I slip my reins a bit since we land on a steep slope downward and have the ditch at the bottom of the slope, a stride away. We're over the vertical and people are starting to applaud as she takes a big skip down the steep landing and leaps across a natural ditch, her studs doing their work to keep her footing. We bound up the other side and she's through. Screams, whistles and applause match the relief in my head, and I am flat on her neck, galloping away, petting her like crazy.

She was in the zone. On the job. No matter how I overrode her the first half, she just kept her cool. I was making errors and she was running like a champion. I decided to get out of her way and treat her like the made horse she suddenly was.

"103 is clear at the coffin! Nicely done, Augusta!" I can hear the smile in the announcer's voice.

My friends were bellowing encouragement and I pick out Ted's voice screaming, clear as a bell, "Kick ON, AUGGIE!!!"

The problem with having a couple really difficult fences on course is that you tend to forget that the other fences aren't to be laughed at either. And, it wasn't that I had done that, but when more than half a division has falls at a fence like the coffin, you are uber focused on your ride there. I was also aware I had thrown aside Plan B. We were in it now and I didn't mean to let her down in the back half.

On over a breather fence and then another pretty serious question of staying on a line while jumping a five foot drop and one stride to a maximum height vertical skinny in the apple grove. Friends had gone through and missed the line, taking out the flags left and right or brushing off the skinny face entirely and running out. They were good riders.

Auggie slows for the approach to the drop. Again, I rely on how fast she packages, shortening her stride to a very bouncy show jump stride. I remind myself to keep my hands low, not take her eye off the vertical in front of her and sit softly and quietly on her back. Auggie bobs her head once looking at the drop before she pulls her knees up and pushes off into space. I open my reins slightly left and right to help keep her straight for the one stride where she has to lift up the legs she just landed on and clear the maximum vertical.

We're gone. Not even a close call. She lands a little under-engined from the effort and I allow her two or three strides to recuperate, breathe and move herself back into rhythm at her own pace. We needed to be sharp, but we didn't need to be fast. I let her rev back up on her own time conscious of getting her home safely and with plenty of gas in the tank. More huge pats on her neck and she bobs her head slightly. Embarrassing as it is for some, I talk to my horses quietly a lot on the course and certainly, after a good effort. Slowing down an uber fit, 16.2 or more hands high thoroughbred quickly, or ramping back up to speed quickly or having them idle, is all accomplished much more easily for me when I add my voice. I also praise them vocally and with a hand on their neck. They look for it, they expect it and deserve it. We're three away from the massive ditch and log.

Up the hill to a ditch and wall, landing us in a paddock and we gallop easily to the other fence line and are out the other side. We are on approach to the huge ditch and rail. Cars are lined up along the driveway and the road having heard about the problems at the fence. I barely notice them other than to note they are below my line up of my telephone pole on the horizon.

I'm careful to avoid the Canadian Teal extravaganza by holding my discipline and not sending Auggie. I hold her, in fact, slowing her, waiting for her to take a breath before I re-balance her. We're running downhill to the left even though the fence is to my right. Out of my peripheral vision, I see the hanging tree trunk. I start looking right, bring the mare's shoulders around, close my fingers and hug her with my legs. The telephone pole slides perfectly into the cross hairs of my eyes and I don't leave it. "Turn your toes east and west and find a ventricle…." Tucked in behind her wither with a soft seat and shoulders tall, my heels are jammed down, a little in front of my knee. We've sprung back to full gallop and we're moving. Fast. "Don't over-ride her. Be quiet. Trust her." Auggie never hesitates. She bunches her quarters and we're airborne! Fourteen feet of space and a huge log left behind like it was nothing. Not a bobble. Not a slip. Exactly on our line.

'Good GIRL!!!!!" I burst out relieved, scrubbing her neck and mane. Pride swells in my chest, almost choking me. My fabulous, young mare often disrespected by others because of her naughtiness. But, not today. Today she was running the ball better than Edelman for the Patriots, all the way into the end zone with a hometown crowd. A lesson in excellence. Galloping strongly, efficiently, listening intently to her pilot like a much more experienced horse. Super star. Exactly as I always knew she would. She is having fun now, proud of herself and she gallops away tugging for more rein.

She was also making an idiot of me. I was so worried moving her up to more complexity, more size, more speed, riding like I had the Hounds of the Baskervilles on my heels and she was galloping around like it was nothing. I was so protective of this wild child I had owned since she was two and all the work just manifest itself without my even being aware. She had so often been a little demon at lower levels and clearly today, the course had her attention. I settled in to get her home. On to the second water complex. The footing there was always a bit deep, so I slow way down, mindful of the stress on her legs and let her jump in quietly, canter two strides across and jump out over another split rail vertical. We turn right and head into the last third of the course.

A big brush goes by in stride and I don't make any fuss except to ride her hind legs up the hill and steer, she is flying. I get right off her back, pet her encouragingly and ask for no more pace than she wants to go. Auggie takes the steeplechase fence downhill like a show jump and clears it by a foot then methodically clocks over two more breathers with the same professionalism. I'm still and quiet, making up for my ride in the first half of the course. On to the wave which looks exactly as you might think and then a hillside of people come into view. My eyes go to the flower beds lying beautifully in front of a solid wood wall strewn with pumpkins and corn stalks. The last fence.

I pick a line, steady her for her last jump and canter over it. She is home to the roar of the coffin crowd not twenty yards away and to my friends who are ready to help us get cooled down and listen to the detail that only horsemen love, of every moment on course. I leap from the tack and swing an arm up and over Auggie's neck. She walks blowing a little, bumping me with her forehead. I hug her tight, tug her ear and let friends get in to smoothly take her tack, switch her bridle for a padded halter and swing her cooler over her while I catch my breath. It would be hours before the relief and euphoria of our ride lessened. Auggie had a hoof in the throne room. She was queen. She'd been so much better than I, busy protecting her, worrying about her. And just like that, a great, brave, talented sport horse was made.

While I was still catching my breath, I see a shock of white hair on a face with a big smile, wearing a red shirt and sitting near the finish in a golf cart. Neil was clapping as loudly as anyone on course. I catch his eye, wave and grin. It was all I could do not to curtsey in front of such sporting royalty, even when I had met him several times. Teddy is also running straight at me, oblivious to my sweaty clothing and lifts me in the air for a bear hug. "Fantastic!!" He drops me just as fast to call to Auggie, who stops and drags my friend leading her back to him so Teddy could hug her, making him laugh and me beam.

The feeling of accomplishment that comes from perfect alignment with your partner on any particular day is difficult to describe: Moonshot. Exhilaration. Bliss. Beaming joy. What a milestone for Auggie. I never looked at her the same way again. Always adored for her personality, she had risen to be exactly what I always knew she could and then went even higher. I was exhausted. She was happy. I let my friend continue to walk her for a few minutes but then took her back, loving the feel of her nose tucked against my back and under my arm, like she was just taking a stroll to her paddock.

Unlike Blue post -run, Auggie didn't swagger around and love an audience. What made her happy was being with me. She'd put on her airs above ground again tomorrow and act the diva then, but after cross country, after extreme effort, aside from praise and treats, the only reward she wanted was my undivided attention. Like a first-string horse. And, that's what she got.

After my division finished, the coffin was pulled from the course for the rest of the day, for safety. I thanked my lucky stars again that things had swung our way. I was even able to laugh at the mother of a girl I knew who by simple intonation, managed to convey her absolute shock that Auggie had run around clean in a midst of so many falls by older, more experienced horses and riders. I wasn't shocked. Or insulted. Her daughter had never made a horse in her life, preferring to learn on the backs of old campaigners and that's great too. But, people can be short sighted. Auggie was a great horse. And more than her naughty behavior would have one believe, she was the sum of her trust and love for me. It was really no surprise at all to have had her throw down a confident, solid and professional round. If she could, she'd have said, "Told you so." She'd have told me that even though Blue was sick, we would still have years to go competing if I'd let her be first string. She finished second. At Ledyard.

Never thinking any of our rides could possibly go that well again in our own backyard, Augusta came back the next year and didn't just gallop around the course like she had springs in her sneakers, she won her division with two rails in hand. What an honor it was to ride those two. I have never had more fun in my life. Ever. They are missed every day.

Auggie. Pretty is as pretty does, indeed.

"His neigh is like the bidding of a monarch, and his
countenance enforces homage. He is indeed a horse."
-William Shakespeare

Where in this wide world can man find nobility without pride,
Friendship without envy or beauty without vanity?
Here in the horse, where grace is served with muscle
And strength by gentleness confined.

-Ronald Duncan, "the Horse" 1954.

CHAPTER SEVEN

Grief

It is a known fact that the overproduction of adrenaline can stop blood flow to your ears. So, when I answered my phone in the car early Saturday morning, with: "Grace, what's wrong?" A rush akin to the Hoover dam was already in full roar.

All I knew is that it was a weird time of day for a call from my retired thoroughbred's guardian. Not her pattern. Irregular. Atypical. An outlier call. A weird pulse was banging in my chest and in truth, had grown from a weird discomfort I had woken with that morning, like a prickly shroud on my chest and shoulders. *"By the pricking of my thumbs, something wicked…"* I dismissed it as some new, horrid, encroaching disease of the aging. Instead, it was worse. The low, sad voice of my friend droned like a flat line distress signal. It was all I could hear through the rushing of the dam noise. I understood nothing. I was trying to hear. I knew it was important that I hear but I could not. I willed a new, piercing, persistent high pitch tone to abate. Grace's voice, usually full of life and energy, was below my frequency.

I interrupted: "Wait, what? I can't... hear...Where is he right now?" Somehow my body knew before my brain, that bad news was coming. At some point, I had swerved over and stopped on a back-country road and was repeating, 'What? Where is he?" until I realized I was buffering myself for what I knew was coming. Giving myself time to get ready.

Stop. Be still. Breathe. Quinn. This is going to hurt. Pull yourself together. At that time, that hour, in that voice, I knew he was hurt or sick or ...But I couldn't HEAR what it was.

"Is he alive?" I shout into the car, the same way all deaf people think they will hear if they increase the outgoing sound pressure. The surging waves in my ears relent slowly. How fast can I get to him? Let me get there. I start mentally organizing myself to get to Virginia. Drug him, run an IV, let me get there. Unless it's a broken leg. Or a twisted colic. No suffering. I might not be able to have him wait, if it's bad... He never moves, travels, goes anywhere without me. He'd fret. Let me get there.

Suddenly, I heard it. So quiet. In the pause of my erratic thoughts, it reached me. "He's gone, Ellie."

"Gone?"

"I'm so sorry..."

"What? How? Wh..When? How? I don't...What happened?"

Silence. The phone was connected but neither of us spoke. Grace was crying softly and trying to collect herself before resuming her explanations and I let the silence hang. I was suddenly exhausted. All that adrenaline, gone with two words. Kill shots. He's gone. Quinn is gone. Numbness gratefully starts to bleed from my crown to my toes.

"I'm broken hearted," her voice is slight and babbling rapidly. "I thought I'd have him for another ten years. Toby is on his last legs, I thought it was going to be Toby. I was ready for it. Never thought it could be him..." she refers to her thirty-one year old darling of a pinto who roams her property at will, hard of hearing, lame, halt and almost blind.

Knowing Quinn, who is very interactive, funny and charming if he trusts you, which he came to do with Grace, it is even worse for her. I have been Quinn's trustee for eleven years, eight of which I saw him everyday. But, of late, when he could be without me and not fret, I had retired him to gorgeous acres of Kentucky blue grass, a best friend and Grace. I visited regularly, but she was now handling him every day. I already had practice missing him. She did not.

Grace had done exactly as I asked and was not insulted that he didn't love her right away, that he snapped his ears back at her or didn't want her too close. She waited. He eventually believed in her because finally, in his later years, he began to trust that he would never be left in bad hands. I transitioned him and he understood. Grace watched how I handled him and knew he could be loving and affectionate and funny. Really funny. Lucille Ball funny- if she could have been a gelding. Ever smart. So, Grace, a great horsewoman, waited. Operating calmly around him. Never staying longer than to perform whatever he needed, respectfully. With caring. Not her ways or schedules, but his. He came to love her for it.

He was a difficult horse because he had a tough start as a youngster and as much as he thought he wanted a solitary existence, he wasn't suited to being "sole survivor" on an island, away from humans. He was a high maintenance guy. He needed extras to thrive. Some horses go out on grass and couldn't care less when they see you again. Quinn needs someone around three o'clock every afternoon to spend a little time. Acknowledge him. He needed grooming, clothes for every season, especially heavy clothes in winter for his sensitive back, a hot meal, warm water to drink in bad weather and he needed some discussion. He wanted to know people come for him every day and that they genuinely had feeling for him. Without that feeling, he was armored. To me, these things for him were as natural as breathing. Quinn. I have a flash of him holding my ponytail gently or my jacket sleeve while I fill his water buckets. We laughed every day.

When he came to me, I ignored a lot of his wild behavior. And he had plenty. The dangerous stuff, I just made hard for him to do, but the other aggressive behaviors were ignored. The worse he was, the nicer I was. If the vet or blacksmith needed to come, I would leave work and be with him so no one corrected him but me. And anyone handling him knew my rules. If they were going be impatient, they needn't appear. It was a long, slow, physical and mental rehab. It's also how I came to spend time every day, talking to him while I leaned back on his shoulder, feeding him apples. Finally, after a few months, he would hook me with his long neck and put me on his shoulder himself, ears pricked happily forward, calm, relaxed and he'd be still, plucking bites of fruit from my hand, slowly chewing them as I muttered stories to him or told him my assessment of his behavior that day. Even when he'd been ghastly, we both found it funny by day's end.

He hadn't received the extras he needed at the first retirement place I had tried and once I realized it on an unannounced visit, he was moved. This time, I visited even more up front, watched his progress and Grace is a thoughtful friend, I knew she'd care honorably for him. Inevitably, they two became good friends.

"What happened?" I asked dully, staring at the largest tree trunk I've seen in a long while beside the nose of my car. Bark is quite interesting, actually. Like skin and veins...The droning alarm is subsiding in my ears. An unwanted memory flash of people running in to pull me away from my father and the hand I was holding tightly in ICU. He disappeared in a swarm of white coats. I already know Quinn's scenario is catastrophic and don't want to hear more. I want to study bark. No Zumba, no talking, no being today.

Grace drew in a steadying breath and started back in: "Of all the calls I never wanted to make. I always wondered what I could possibly say...I know how much he loved you and you him. I loved watching him with you. I wish all my owners cared so m—"

'It's ok, Gracie. Tell me. What happened?" I interrupt in a monotone.

"I blanketed him up because it was about 30F last night and he took his evening treat normally, had eaten a good dinner and was with Odie, happily mowing some fresh spring grass. They wanted to stay out. The vet just saw him 10 days ago...."

"It's ok. I know. Keep going."

"Early this morning, I was pouring coffee into "go" cups for Chris and me, when I looked out of the window and saw Odie standing still over Quinn, who was lying down. He never lies like that." Her voice cracks before she resumes. "Odie was standing still as a statue, not grazing, not moving, head hanging over Quinn. We tore out there and he was gone. Odie was guarding him. We had to move him aside; he didn't want to leave him." She bursts into soft, hitching sobs.

Odie, a huge 17 h.h. ex-show jumper with a fiery red coat, was Quinn's best friend and had been since the day he first arrived at Grace's. He had made him welcome and became his instant confidante. SNL's Wayne and Garth. Their stalls were next to one another and they went everywhere together. The hunormous, chunky, kind, red warmblood with the smaller, slim, grey thoroughbred. Friendship didn't come easily to Quinn who was very picky about which horses he liked. Which people he liked. Most could come or go. Odie, he loved. He was a Godsend. They were as close as brothers. He was going to have a couple bad days, too. It's always the ones we leave behind who suffer. Christ, poor, lovely Odie...

I'm staring at my tree bark, watching the patterns made from the depressions between the skin of strained wood that splits and spreads as it grows, climbing upward and out to the slimmer branches and how the strands of wood smoothly reshape into one skin again. Bumps, holes, aberrations are smoothly glossed over with time. New growth around a lost limb finds its way upward tenaciously but depending at which point the trunk is wounded, it might arrest growth completely. The goal of summiting to the sky creates innovative formations on the trunk skin, accommodating growth, disease or death.

Like a family. My bark was getting a cut-back. Stunted endings. Part of a life's work, I suppose. Things end. The cornucopia of directions we support also, inevitably, narrow and end.

Grace's voice pierces my consciousness again: "I don't know when it happened. We saw him minutes before dark for night check last night. I don't know what happened. The vet is on his way."

"Describe his body to me, please. Everything. What was the turf around him like? Everything, Grace, please."

Her voice shook and I stared at my tree outside the car like it had some properties that would eliminate the last ten minutes like magic if I looked hard enough. If Jack and a random beanstalk could create magic, maybe, so could I. I thought I might lose Quinn when his other lifelong friend, Africa died. I moved him to Grace's then, stayed with him the week and transferred him into Odie's care.

I just wanted to say goodbye.

It doesn't matter how many pass on before or, how many times we lay our pets to rest, it is not a task that lightens with repetition. I am also one of those who feels it badly. I remembered being horrified, two weeks after my mother had died, when I was operating normally and allowing life to drag me on, nine days after my reconstituting five day rule, to find that I was silently weeping still when I had chanced to have dinner out with a close friend. Water just poured down my cheeks and I could do nothing about it. Nothing. I'm not a weeper. I stayed home other than for work for another two weeks, to make sure I appeared myself in public.

I listened more and Grace's voice came clearer instead of the pounding noise of blood in my ears. "His head is laying down hill about 20 feet from the hillside run-in shed in that field. His blanket has shifted up on his neck a bit and he has a swelling there from the buckle, I think, I don't think he could have choked himself…"

"Probably because his weight was pointed downward. Lower neck? Between his chest?" I interrupt monotone, seeing him as I speak...

"Yes," She is trying to get her emotions under control again.

"What else? Turf?"

"The turf was undisturbed."

'You looked as far as fifteen feet all around him?"

"Yes."

"Wounds, blood, grass stains?" My voice is low and mechanical. Quinn is, was, a gray. If he struggled, if he was wrestling around in pain, he'd show it.

"Just the small lump where the blanket buckle must have jammed into his lower neck with the pressure of his body position. I'm so worried the blanket choked him but I can't imagine ..."

"Gracie, " I say calmly, "I'm sure that wasn't it. Please, just tell me what you see."

"Ok. He's positioned downhill, as I said. Legs look fine, hooves, neck except for that swelling at the buckle. No grass stains but…" she stops.

"Say it. Whatever it is. It's ok. Say it…"

"There was blood in his nostrils," her voice shook and was so low, I found myself wondering why my ears were recruiting suddenly – sound was so sharp, it was painful. I could hear a pin drop.

"How much? In both?"

"Yes, in both. Not like he bled out there, but a trickle in both." Her voice hitches and I hear her breathing to balance it.

I feel completely still. Defeated. There are no magic beans in this story. Core heavy, extremities prickling. He's gone. *By the pricking of my thumbs*…More than anything else she had said, that picture slammed into my head and I could see him. He left. Please, let it have been easy for him.

The sound I know so well of his heartbeat booms in my ears. Eight powerful beats every fifteen seconds. I always had a small suspicion that Quinn's bad days, his reluctant behavior in certain things, might be from something we were all missing and I'd use my mother's stethoscope to listen to him occasionally after work. Huge swishing in …and out…I feel him exactly as I always did, ribs rising and falling against my side, warmth seeping into my bones as I pressed against him listening, an arm up and over his withers to the other side of his back. I would lean fully against him for minutes and he'd not move a muscle while I listened. It made him still. For a bit of a prickly horse, he loved hugging.

What bliss it had been, to have him at home and come from dinner to stop in the barn for night check. Sometimes, still in evening clothes, I'd stand in his stall, pumps or sling-backs buried in a foot of sweet-smelling pine shavings, leaning on his shoulder while he ate his treats. If he was happy, I was happy. He'd curl his long neck completely around me and quietly listen to me tell him how great he'd been that day while he took raisins or mints or an apple from my palm. Eyes soft and completely relaxed in his spotless stable, seeing him with his best friend next door and how secure and happy they were, was serenity. Better than any hot toddy before bed. Unlike the rest of the day, last check at bedtime was completely calm. Tranquil. As was his mood. My nervous little monster. Calm and happy at bedtime. Always. He never ate apples or carrots in two bites but would eat them like I did. Piece after piece. God, I love the smell of horsehair. Wet, dry, I loved how he smelled.

"Ellie?"

"Sorry. Yes?"

"I want you to know the vet is on the way. And we'll find out what happened. He's been perfectly happy and healthy up until..."

"Grace, please text me a picture of him as he is. And have the vet call me when he's had a chance to have a look. No one is to touch him without my express permission for an autopsy. It sounds like a sudden heart event to me. But let's wait for the vet." My voice is low but steady. "I don't want him going through - I don't want him touched... Let's get feedback from the vet, first, but I'd rather he not be disturbed unless he finds something out of the ordinary. I really appreciate the transparency."

I have to get off the phone. Like a runaway freight train coming, I feel the urgency to be quiet.

'Thank you, Gracie, for everything you've done. I have to go. I need an hour. I'll come back with you. I'm sorry. I know you cared for him and you see, saw him everyday. I'm sorry for you, too. Kiss Odie for me. Tell him "Thank you."

It must be November not March, I think to myself. Everything I see is gray. Like an old, foreign film. I must be blind as well as deaf. There's movement around me but I see no color and I feel nothing. There is nothing so isolating as pain.

"Of course. I have no words. I loved him too. I can't believe it. It's such a shock," Grace breaks off in tears.

I'm torn between the colorful picture show running in my mind,which I could stay in forever with Quinn, and registering the bleak reality around me. He left and I wasn't with him. He's gone. With no one around him but Odie. Please don't let him have suffered. I have to think a minute. Be still a minute. Poor Odie.

Mechanically I soothe his handler for the past 2 years. "I know. He knew. I appreciate it. He trusted you. I can't thank you enough for all you've done for him. I'm sorry I can't stay on. I'll call in a bit. Please, have the vet call." I repeat.

"Of course. I'm so sorry. He loved you so much. Please remember he went to bed fine last night. Whatever it was, it was fast." She can't stop, really. And I can't listen for any longer.

"Ok. Thanks, Grace." The tone, volume and rhythm of my voice is dead.

I press a button on the steering wheel, disconnecting and realize I'm still staring at the tree. I'm supposed to be meeting people in now, five minutes. I don't want to do anything or see anyone. I want to be in my house. The insult of life begins. I make a call begging off, barely aware of what I was saying and hang up. A couple texts and calls ring in and I ignore them. Shouldn't things just stop? Can't they just stop for a month maybe, five days, five minutes? I just need to sort myself out.

When my father died, and he was my first parent to go, I just could not believe life went on. Days clicked by at exactly the same rate while I was frozen in place. I just couldn't figure out what had happened. Where was he? How would I feel his thoughts? His voice? I was *not* ready. It was marginally better for my mother, but watching people you love leave you, each in their own different way, is surely the worst thing we endure on earth. Really, things should stop until you right yourself. Just a little time until you become aware of balance again in the realm. I had two days before work resumed. I guess that was a small blessing.

> Stop all the clocks, cut off the telephone,
> Prevent the dog from barking with a juicy bone,
> Silence the pianos and with muffled drum
> Bring out the coffin, let the mourners come...
> The stars are not wanted now; put out every one:
> Pack up the moon and dismantle the sun;
> Pour away the ocean and sweep up the woods:
> For nothing now can ever come to any good.
> *-WH Auden. Funeral Blues.*

One of my favorite poems. We'd have been friends, Auden and I.

Sadly though, the clock never stops. And people's expectations of what you normally are, they never change. Some people are simply not blessed with knowing and connecting with these athletic, noble, intelligent animals, didn't consider them family, and so I was well used to the masquerade. One wants to fit in, of course – so strangers could never know. I am a private person by nature and of all things, grief is intensely personal. Some need to vent it out loud, others carry it quietly, heavily. I had to prepare for it. Carry myself the same way, get through regular days dodging verbal body blows by gleaning past people, keeping to myself, speaking nothing of it for the cushion of a few days.

Five day rule was ticking. Think anything and do anything I needed for five days and then eyes forward. It won't feel good for a long time, but act your way to normalcy. I know I take it badly. My greatest friends know I take it badly. I cannot dial even one of them yet. These investments of love and time and the outdoors with your best quadruped friends in shared adventure can't be shrugged off at whim. At least, not by me. They are the timekeepers of our lives. The names on our personal eras. Mirrors of escapades and meaningful time shared. Reflections of happiness. I'm grateful he was safe until he left me. And, I'm grateful my pets do not survive me, or imagine their distress and potentially, their change in circumstance. Hadn't that always been the goal for Quinn? Making sure he never was in risky circumstances again?

It wasn't that I took him and imagined he was a competitive project. Those days, those years were the best of years. But, we move on. He was a rehab project I loved. One can give to one hundred non-profits and walk away or you can find a meaningful project and stand up for them. Quinn, unhappy and lost in his own head. He was just six years old when I took him.

I needed to be happy that at least, he was his authentic self when he died. Happy, calm, loving. Safe. These horrible ruptures in the fabric of one's life are painful to repair. A place or piece of me, where I am also my authentic self, tore away. It takes huge effort to not let it show. The devastation. The loss of something dear. I'm never very good at it. I'm not sure I'd like to be one of those who is. These are the days that I understand why some just ride the emotional middle. It's hard work to open yourself up and take life's hits full frontal. No one likes it.

I realize the car is still on, idling on the side of a road. Right then, it seemed a complicated ordeal for me to know how to get home. Be alone. Not in public. People would say the polite things and I'd not be wanting to hear. They didn't know him. They can't imagine the brain that existed with even more agility than his body. They do not know the bond that exists. I didn't have the desire or energy to have to explain it. And explain I would have to, with my face petrified into granite. Telling those who did understand would augment my pain for now. I realize I hear nothing, again. Deaf.

What a change eleven years makes. Was it even possible? The same beautifully bred, gorgeous but angry horse who almost bit one of my fingers right off the second day I owned him, is the same one who runs - ran, away from friends or whatever he was doing, the second he heard my whistle; the same one who would rather follow me around his paddock with his nose lightly holding my shirt between his teeth, listening to me scold him for losing another shoe, than graze or be with his pals; the same one who guarded me in the barn from people coming too close like a comically large German Shepherd. Finally, unafraid himself, he always wanted to protect me, yanking me sideways onto his shoulders and snaking his head as far as the cross ties would let him, at whomever he didn't trust around us. The same one who would slap down first one foreleg, then the other, out in front of him on the cross ties, so I could groom it for him and he could curl himself over me and amuse himself taking out my ponytail elastic – very carefully.

He should have been mowing a field until he was 30. Blue passed away at 31 and had been riddled with way more severe medical issues and survived them. He was the first to survive EPM in the country thanks to Cornell University Veterinary School and their team of cutting age vets. My champion, fought through a disease they now finally have a vaccine for, and made it to thirty-one having been owned only by three different women in his life, all of whom adored him.

Quinn. Silvercap. Fat, happy, calm at last. From one wrong situation to another for his first six years, furious and hating people before coming to me and being happy. Gone at seventeen. It was a personal honor to have stepped in for this horse of such immense intelligence who I knew only briefly during his first six years. Every day he showed me what a difference it made to him. A little kindness. A little, well, a lot of patience. A hack here or there was all I saw of him as a baby while I was living out of state studying. He was so nervous all the time, teeth chattering, feet dancing, eyes shifting all over that my heart bled for him. I could literally see him think. He was so exceptionally bright. So bright it was a crime to watch people not hear him or listen to him; be deaf to him.

The racetrack would have been a very scary place for him. The frantic activity every day, multiple people coming and going in your personal space using pitchforks to move you around, the nervous energy all the babies exude, constant movement, cacophony of noises on race day, everyone's pulse around you at the heights of stress. Some love it, some don't. He didn't. Break, bend left and go from dead still to flat gallop. Do it better and faster the next day.

No matter how splashy, tough and huge the attitude he fronted, gaining anything "fast" from him was going to come from slowing down. So handsome, everything early in his life as it can be for youngsters, was too fast for him. He was moved off the track where he didn't want to run, into show jumping when he barely understood his own balance. Already fearful and nervous of being asked what he could not give every day, his fighting grew. Not a conformist, not clear about his understanding of humans, hugely prideful, the clashing in his mind was perfectly visible to me. I never saw him but for hearing some story from a groom or barn manager that he was 'coming along' but a tough one, usually told to me while he rested his head in my hands or while we walked out of the stable yard for a hack with him calm and flat footed.. But that was before he went south.

There is such a thing as some instant bond of the mind and just like with Auggie, when she was in distress and a baby, it came alive again with Quinn. He was frantically busy at something all the time. In his own head. Worried sick. Acting like all this never bothered him. Acting so tough. Trying to remove himself mentally from wherever he was, then girding himself for a fight he knew was coming when people tried to bring him back. Had he been a small boy, he'd have run around with his fingers in his ears screaming in your face, willing you away. It was transparent to me. Surely, they would all see that. Slow him down. Fix his body pain. SLOW. Repair his trust.

What pride this lovely horse had. In the end, when they were doing things to push him and force him for sale out of state, denying him food, leaving him out overnight, jumping his legs off with sore back and ankles, doing things that made me sick to hear when I came back to take him, they had tried everything to break him, weaken his will, make him conform just to be monetized and he just wouldn't do it. He simply never liked how they asked him. He never liked that they didn't listen to him. He tried. There were obviously reasons he couldn't easily respond the way some others do. The answer to a lot of those questions may now lie simply in what seemed a faulty heart. No one listened.

Money is a great motivator. It can also corrupt good intention. There is a lot of it in this sport. Breeders can breed and raise babies as nicely as they ought, but once they leave their hands, it's a crap shoot for the animal. Quinn had lovely breeders. They always try to keep an eye on their babies and get them secure. Quinn slipped through the cracks on his crooked road to finding a profession.

The day I came to collect him and take him home with me, he was six years old, emaciated, head hanging, skin mottled and a mess from fungus, lame and he hated people more than he could ever say but when I sadly looked into his stall and saw him snake his neck around, slap his ears back against his neck hatefully, our eyes met. I saw him. And he was in there. The little 4 year old I bonded with right away just hacking with friends a few times. The nervous baby. Six years old now. Too much for an amateur to handle, no way for a professional to get their money out, bred of the best blood in American racing and there he was, shattered. No one had cared what he thought. No one listened. I was told by a good friend that he was back and needed someone. He didn't have many options left to him so, I went to get him.

The last thing I was told before I loaded him to take him to his new home, was from a woman I knew distantly. She had run a stable on a farm nearby and had eventually found her way into a trainer position in the void of truly excellent horsemen moving further south with the circuit or retiring.

"You don't want to feed this one," she replied when I asked what his food regimen was. She whispered to me conspiratorially, like we were great friends: "He's a bastard, this one. Food will make him worse. Trust me, you don't want to give him more food." Standing in the barn aisle listening to Bastard or whatever name they called him, frantically slap his right foreleg on the cement, pawing and pawing and seeing his frantic eye was turning my eye on her to black. OCD, lost in his head, panicked, starving he was pawing the air at chest height and then slamming his poor shod foot on the concrete, smack, Smack , SMACK!

"I actually do want to feed him. What are you giving him?" I repeat coldly, knowing I needed the information to transition him onto a better diet without aggravating his stomach. No more stress for this horse. No more.

"He gets a quart at night of high fat, low energy mix and hay." She says defensively into my dead eyes. "I'll get some ready then, for a day or two for…."

"He's seventeen hands and ONE quart? Don't bother. I'm loading. I'll see to him."

It's all I can do to shut my mouth, spin on my heel and keep my pulse low for Quinn, and leave without getting into a contentious argument that wouldn't do either him or me any good.

Her day would come and it did several years later, when she was silly enough to stop by my trailer at a horse show and scornfully commented with tons of people we know in common around, "I see you finally gave up on that nasty little grey horse you picked up from me, eh? Who's this one? He's lovely. I told you, the other one was a bastard, not worth the effort. I tried to warn you…" she prattled on patronizingly until I felt my molars start to grind.

I breathed in slowly and kept a half smile on my lips. Quinn was staring at me, eyes on, while he methodically tore clumps of grass, grazing while we waited to get ready for show jumping. I kept my pulse low so he stayed relaxed knowing any sudden reaction and he'd drag me clear across the field, sitting as I was on an upturned muck basket like a bad pony-clubber. My smile broadened as I stared at him, huge, muscled, glossy and dead calm after cross country, mowing the field around me on his lead like a giant dog.

I had been talking with friends when she appeared around the back of the trailer and turned my body fully now toward Quinn, watching for signals that he was going to react as negatively to her voice as I was. He never acknowledged her, other than to maintain eye contact with me and keep eating, alert to any movement I might make. He heard her though. His focus on me told me that. My heart swelled as usual, with the totality of his trust in me. He had not a worry in his head after three years. But he wasn't taking his eye off me. There was sudden silence in our previously cheery, chatty little group of about twelve riders, all catching up, all who knew her.

I took my time turning back to stare at her, a small smile on my lips but eyes so flat I could feel them heavily in my face. The silence was getting uncomfortable for everyone. Anyone who knew me could see my demeanor had changed and I was in no mood to play nice or dignify this woman with an appearance of liking her. Pistols at dawn. She long deserved a public dressing down for what she was. What she did. My friends were either rearing back, waiting for the verbal knife throwing to start, or they were starting to laugh nervously at the sight of her even talking to me.

Civility is important so it's easy to float by these people you are not fond of and say little. But, even then, I knew there were surely horses in her stable who leaped for the back of their stalls at mealtime instead of hanging their heads into the hallway in happy anticipation. That knowledge is harder to float by. Her mistake was to stop and another to presume she knew anything about Quinn or me.

The slower I move, the softer I speak, the larger the chance that I am readying myself for a bloodletting. I was fiercely protective of Quinn. It was hard to remember more than a couple times I've ever been that upset in the past ten years. Two of my friends with me had seen Quinn when he'd been at this woman's barn. They, like me, were not laughing a bit. We were at a friend's farm competing though, someone I respect and care for and so I lowered my eyes to smile broadly again at Quinn and remind myself elegance is a way of thought. She was nothing. More, I knew our success at this teeniest of shows was making her nuts.

Until that moment, I had not even thought of being there to win. We came to play and have fun and Quinn loved it. That he was doing so well was merely icing on the cake. Quinn was kicking on like he should have really been two levels above what he was competing. We were having a ball. But, now, I was looking even more forward to show jumping with my horse who used to rear straight up on end at the sight of a colored rail and who had already performed brilliantly in the first two phases of his first horse trial.

" Yes, it's been a great day. It's just fun to be out doing a little stuff when I don't really compete anymore. He seems to like it. Point and shoot. He can't wait to gallop on to the next..." I hear my friends getting even more quiet behind me if that was possible, knowing I was letting out the hook and line.

"Yes," she interrupts. "I saw you galloping through the water and over the wall. He looks so sweet too, bobbing his head when you pet him, lovely expression, great gallop. He's lovely. Where did you find him? she pushes.

"Thank you. I love him. He's been a pleasure. A kindred spirit." I'm standing up now and have placed an arm over Quinn's back while he eats. I paused for a long, slow, beat while I scratch his withers. Then in the silence, with almost everyone we know listening, there was Quinn's moment:

"He's actually not new. This IS Quinn, or whatever you called him in your stable. Same horse. I just decided to ignore you and feed him. Surely you recognize horses you've handled in your own barn?" A fake smile curves my lips but there is no mistaking the disgust in my eyes or in my quiet, even words. One of the hardest things I have to do is to not allow my emotions to transcribe on my face. That day, in that moment, I purposefully let them rip.

I watched color bleed into her cheeks, her eyes open wide and her jaw slacken in shock as she snapped her head around to stare over at Quinn's dappled, glossy, round belly, his snowy coat and his side – eye, as he continued to mow the field beside me. I wait another beat before I continued slowly, "Oh, do be a little careful coming too close around the rig here. You know those bastards… really long legs and really long memories." I wink and smile.

I can say quite honestly, I have never been one of those riders who finds it amusing to throw veiled insults to others having a better or worse round than I or who may have better or worse talent then me. I've been on the receiving end frequently, it's part of competition, but I just have no interest. Most riders in my circle were successful, were friends, and we supported each other. I always stayed focused on competing with myself so never felt I needed to be rude or petty. But, I really don't like horsemen who don't respect horses. It's a fissure in my veneer. It overrides everything. When do we stand up for important things? When is it really convenient? Rarely. But there she appeared, at our dueling appointment, unprovoked, slandering Quinn. Even competitors who had no idea of Quinn's history but knew us were stopped, aware of some awkward situation unfolding. Awkward for her. I was enjoying myself.

"Thanks for stopping by. See you out there." I turned dismissively and pulled two pink mints from my britches' pocket and watched Quinn devour them happily and gum my white show shirt with pink sugar.

I've never seen her again since, when she didn't lower her eyes and try to run the other way. Smarter than she looks, in the end.

But back then, it just reinforced that I could not have lived with myself if I hadn't taken him. I remembered how my Dad used to say, 'They find you," while shaking his head in dismay. I was working full time, I didn't need an upper level event horse anymore, I had no time for it. But I had the time for this emaciated, vicious, nervous wreck of a youngster. He just needed his person. So, I took him on. All the fundraising in the world that I have done which I always hope goes to good cause is great, but here stood a deserving recipient right in front of me, when I no longer was competing, when my goals were very different in life and when I would be happy for time with him, off on my own as usual, doing another work project. It had been literally a matter of life and death for him. I knew him. How could I turn my back?

Sure, I could have bought a horse I could compete and enjoy training every day at my old level of riding, but I've had those days. I've been blessed with the best of training and travel and competition with the best of friends along with me. Nothing will be the same as that. It also takes absolute focus to reward the effort and expense. Choosing Quinn was much the same way you'll hear, "it's as easy to love a rich man as a poor one." Sure, but decency, in face of the ones with great potential but no money, in face of a connection you know to magically exist, should prevail over no connection and cash, any day. It rarely does, but it should. Doing the right thing should prevail.

My days were immersed in business after my graduate degree and my body and pocketbook hadn't quite recovered. Quinn required a year of vet oversight and treatments while we determined what hurt and how to get rid of inflammation, but he was nothing like the expense of keeping competition horses on the road in the peak of fitness and training. I slowly got fit again as well, transitioning from constant, immobilizing disc issues in my back by acquiring a much stronger core riding. If there ever was a good cause to give back to, after all the sport I've enjoyed, lovely friends I've acquired and fabulous memories I've made, it was Quinn. Elite Kentucky blood cursing through his veins, but so much pride, he'd die before lowering his head in response to the pushing or disrespect we can see in this industry. It is easy to forget horses have career paths, too. And they are not always aligned or suited with what their humans want to do. There are so many great people who love horses in this sport. I feel strongly about pushing back against the few who are not.

One of my friends told me when Quinn was gone, "You always laughed at him when other trainers would choose to "correct" him and he loved you and listened to you for it." It was true.

There is usually a reason if you have a big fighter on your hands. Body pain, mental anguish, medical issue. Something. You must have trust and liking between you before anyone can hear a discussion, let alone a correction. True of humans as much as for animals. The more I knew him, the better I could hear him. The more I could hear, the more he calmed down and could listen. It goes two ways.

After a very hard first year, some might say a dangerous and difficult first year, (I would be one of those,) we flourished into a new way to communicate and never looked back. I wasn't sure we'd make it while I was starting a business and he required so much attention initially. I was on the phone in horror one night, with one of my best friends after one of Quinn's twenty-minute, quiet walks:

"We walked past a jump standard today and the next thing I knew, he was pawing the air and I don't mean a little lift off the ground, I mean going vertical! I was curled over his withers straight up, praying his balance was as good as he thought it was. I don't like rearers. Being a Stubbs painting, wild horse is one thing, rearing to unseat me is another. Not exactly what I expected, to say the least. All I could think of was him falling backwards and crushing me. I competed for fifteen years and was fine and now -This is how it's going to happen? I'm retired, for heaven's sake!"

But, like any endeavor done well in life, commitment means everything. When you have big challenges, you can't straddle six things and hope the one problem thing will correct itself. I mentally was forging a business and 'not the rider' I had been on the circuit for fifteen years and my mental complacency reflected that. The concentration I had innately always had when I put a foot in a stirrup as a competitive rider, wasn't necessary for a nice rehab horse. So, I thought. While I lay tossing and turning, unable to sleep after that ride, I realized what I was doing and that I had a choice. Move the problem horse on to certain hell on earth or death, or I could decide I *was* the rider I used to be and get on with it. So, I got on with it. I left my office the next day at noon, surprising Quinn (who was very schedule conscious,) tacked up and we began to derive our new blueprint for communication. I concentrated and made sure I stayed two steps ahead of him every...single...ride and simply didn't allow him to be horrid. It took months and patience and scrubbing his withers in disagreements when one's inclination was perhaps, not to do that, until his trust came back and he realized that I wouldn't overreact. But he was also not allowed bad behavior. I just made it impossible for him to do it.

Slowly, we acquired days of laughter and Quinn regained his love of life, a strong and fit body, and became talented in flat work and cross country jumping. Nothing more than his old injuries could stand, just enough to make him proud of himself, shape his lovely body to its peak and make him happy working. When he showed me signs of not wanting to work or that his feet stung jumping, or that he would rather hack than do dressage, that's what we did. He came out the next day and worked harder. He was telling me, no matter how thorough his vet workups were, there was more to his naughty behavior. And I listened.

When he was stronger physically and feeling better and better mentally, he was startled one day, hacking out by a river where he was first boarded. We came around a small S curve in the riverbank and voila! A goose. He swung into half pirouette almost leaving me in the dirt, disappeared under me and was sprinting in full extension towards home in under one second. I have never felt any horse dig in that fast and explode into such intense speed. He almost lost me. It took me a field to get back in the tack properly and another to try to slow him down. I also realized in mid-flight, he was in perfect rhythm. Yes, way too fast, but he was no longer afraid of the goose he saw, (fowl was bad) he was running for fun, stretching his body to the max, loving the speed. When we slowed to a hand gallop, I burst out laughing and scrubbed his neck in awe. "We're going to keep this to ourselves or you'll find yourself back at Belmont next." Quinn blew a little and then walked home happily, swinging his lovely head this way and that, very pleased with himself. I am so protective of where and how my horses move in order to keep them sound, that I had been horrified that he bolted, and then with no other choice but to stick with him, had the most exhilarating thirty seconds I could remember since eventing.

He never trusted anyone but me and recently Grace, in eleven years, but he would at least tolerate obediently anyone who had to handle him and no one handled him whom I was not aware of or who hadn't been schooled precisely on how to care for him in the stables. What more reward can you achieve than to take something so utterly desperate and unhappy and see him become himself again. Kind, loving, loyal, funny and talented.

He died happy, surrounded by people and horses he loved, even if I wasn't there. Another gift from years of trust. We were fiercely loyal to each other. Nothing ever changed that. He knew I loved him all the time and the years we did spend, lucky enough to see each other every single day, lent him confidence recently in his new homes away from home. The short stint in his first retirement place with a woman I'd not call a horsewoman, I moved him from but even those months, he trusted he'd be ok. He trusted that I'd know. And I did.

What I learned from some of these experiences is that there are some ugly manifestations of unhappiness in this world. There are occasionally those who strengthen their need for self-aggrandizement through the disrespect and painful intimidation of animals. Sometimes, it's just for money. Just that simple. Just that sad. We are a disposable nation in a disposable time and these noble warriors, now performance athletes or pets or handicap transport for grateful rehabilitating humans, these constant givers without asking for anything, are disposed of all the time for what I call the Goldilocks syndrome. They are never just "quite right" after being broken over and over by humans.

Most horses in our competitive circle are bred, ridden and trained by reputable and excellent horsemen and are usually blessed to be cared for in the style which they deserve. Respect flows two ways. If you want their best in a tough spot in competition, it should be muscle memory from all they know of you, to give it to you. It's the difference between winning and losing some days. Between a smooth ride and a crash, a lot of days.

Our horses' expectations are a lot to live up to, but the rewards are a ridiculous overflow of riches. Good horse people yearn for our hands in horsehair like spring air to our lungs and do our honorable best for creatures who need it. As Churchill is famously quoted to say, "The outside of a horse is good for the inside of a man." How very true, certainly in my case. If we don't do right by those who must rely on the supposed raised intelligence of their human partners for patience and guidance and help, then what are we, really?

Dogs and horses have added the sparklers to the cake of my everyday life for as long as I have memory. They are the natural adapters on earth. The ones who see bright lights ahead and keep trusting, learning, communicating and trying to get us to connect and hear their intelligence. The ones waiting to be allowed as much happiness and personal success as their potential and handlers will lend. Just like we all should want for each other. The joy and positive lessons they spread are immense. I never laugh more than I do with my horses or dogs. They are communicating all the time but you have to have ears wide open to listen and truly enjoy the symphony.

A ball bounces past my tree trunk and my picture show jerked to a stop, interrupting my thoughts. I'm still sitting, engine humming, numb. I stare at my left index finger against the steering wheel. I had been cussing to myself lately that it ages my hand with its crooked, arthritic bump on the last joint, twisting a bit to the left, remnant of day two with Quinn when he almost snapped it right off, biting it to the bone and then some. It is the first time in the past hour that the corner of my mouth tilts upward. I suddenly think my stiff, crooked finger looks just right. The pain that resides there is nothing anymore.

Quinn's beautiful face appears right in front of me, eyes soft, ears pricked alertly forward. I see him so sharply that I feel my chest hollow out in yearning to touch him just once more, stroke his cheeks and kiss his soft muzzle goodbye. I'm frozen, afraid he'll disappear before I can brand the details of what I feel when I see him, into "forever" memory. Never would I forget his likeness. I have kept him in my mind for eleven years. I would recognize him in the dark, from a half mile away or painted a different color. It is the awe, the joy, the calm I feel with him that I am already afraid to forget. Never a bad day.

For such a gorgeous creature, he had the lowest, most gravelly voice when he whickered for me and the highest piercing scream if he was worried. He'd knock me flat and run to avoid fowl of any size. No one was faster, getting into everything or anything piled near him. In a blink, he'd be throwing things left and right as fast as I was picking them up. How accident prone he was. How he'd love to hold the back of my shirt and walk around the fields with me looking for one of his lost shoes. How fast he'd come over the hill in the paddock when he heard my car and how everyday, he had enormous interest in "fixing" my pony-tail holders. Heaven help you if you forgot to dress him and there was mud. Your ride time would be cut in half while you uncovered the rest of him painstakingly with multiple brushes when the only white things left on him when you had arrived, were his eyes. He really loved a hot shower and hated a cold one. Every pair of my breeches went through laundry with pink mints in the pockets. He loved forever those who meant something to him, Africa, Odie, me. How enormously smart he was.

I draw in my breath, tilt my chin toward the sky and blow softly, sending a last, long exhale upwards into his huge, seeking nostrils, waiting, hoping I will feel him blow softly back, the way we always said goodnight. I half lift a hand from the steering wheel, but he's already disappearing.

Godspeed, sweet boy. Safe travel. I will always hear you and I will always miss you.

"I know how much you loved him and he you. You performed miracles with that horse. It was an education for anyone that knew him before you. Your relationship was the finest example of trust I've ever seen. He's grazing in the big pasture now, watching you make your way to him." A friend.

Acknowledgements

Dedication
To my beloved mother,
who thought I was never listening.

I owe a special debt of gratitude to Dana Dikaitis, this book's lavishly talented designer and Sherry Brydon, horse-mad girls and now accomplished career women, whose unfailing enthusiasm, friendship and support throughout this project have been deeply appreciated. To my friend, Jack Murray, student of American Academy of Art and the School of the Art Institute of Chicago, professor Emeritus at Endicott College 1959 - 1995, artist and horseman, who at 92 still unites us all with his own love of life, all things horses and who generously and beautifully illustrated this book. Notable mention goes to all my riding friends from camp who were silly enough to keep telling me they liked my stories! I wish to thank Alexandra Dane, the spine in any adventure worth doing, for her unflinching support and aptitude for herding wandering words back on track. A full-bodied, heart-felt thank you to my professional friends who supported this endeavor in any and every way!
None of these stories would have been memorable at all if not for my great coaches and friends - what a blessing it was to ride and laugh with the very best.
Lastly, the lion's share of my gratitude goes to the real Artemus Gordon, Blue Boy, Augusta, Quinn, Gem, Sam, Huck, Justin, Maverick, Queeny, Tasha, Niko, Balthazar and Ricky who gave me fur friends, courage and days that exceeded even my greatest aspirations of joy.